# MIND OVERCOMING ITS CANKERS

An In-depth Study of Mental Effluents in the Buddhist Perspective

by

VENERABLE ACHARYA BUDDHARAKKHITA

Buddhist Publication Society
P.O. Box 61
54, Sangharaja Mawatha
Kandy,
Sri Lanka

Revised edition 2004 (5000 copies)

National Library of Sri Lanka -
Cataloguing-in-Publication Data

Acharya Buddharakkhita Thera
Mind overcoming its cankers / Acharya
Buddharakkhita Thera - Kandy:
Buddhist Publication Society, 2004 - 230 pp.;
22 cm.
ISBN 955-24-0250-6
i. 294.3823 DDC 21 ii. Title

1. Sutrapitaka 2. Buddhism - Sacred books

ISBN 955-24-0250-6

*Printed by :*
**Ajith Printers**
85/4 Old Kesbewa Road,
Gangodawila, Nugegoda.
Sri Lanka.
Tel : 011-4303917

# Contents

# PREFACE
## TO THE FIRST EDITION

"Spiritual deliverance," says the Buddha, "is attained by the destruction of the mental cankers." Indeed, the Arahat is referred to as *khiṇāsava*, the canker-freed one. A seeker of Truth, therefore, should know what these cankers are, and what he should do to rid himself of them. The answer lies in the *Sabbāsava Sutta*, wherein the Enlightened One unfolds a methodology which in its application is totally effective.

With this profound Sutta as the basic theme, materials were collected from various sources scattered in the Pāli canon to present a reasonably comprehensive study of the subject. Explicit and implicit references to the cankers are an integral part of the Pāli *Tipiṭaka*. Only those texts and commentaries that elaborate on and elucidate the nature of cankers and the methods of their elimination were drawn upon. An exhaustive catalogue of allusions to cankers would amount to a mere academic exercise, and would serve no purpose.

It is earnestly hoped that this work will be used as a practical guide to self-improvement, inner peace and liberation from a world that is increasingly becoming entangled in false values.

May this humble offering be a flower at the feet of the Enlightened One, its true author.

May all beings be happy!

Ven. Acharya Buddharakkhita.
Maha Bodhi Society,
Bangalore, 1978.

# PREFACE
# TO THE REVISED EDITION

"Mind Overcoming its Cankers" is an in-depth study of mental effluents in the Buddhist perspective. The first edition of this book was brought out in 1978 by the Buddha Vacana Trust, Mahā Bodhi Society, Gandhinagar, Bangalore. In 1994 a reprint of this edition was brought out by Buddhist Wisdom Centre, Petaling Jaya, Selangor, Malaysia, for free distribution. In 2003 a Vietnamese translation of this book was produced by the Tathāgata Meditation Center, San Hose, California, USA, also for free distribution. A revised edition of the book has now been prepared which the BPS, Kandy, Sri Lanka is publishing. We thank all those who have helped in the publication of the Second edition of this book.

This is an Author's humble offering at the lotus feet of the Tathāgata Buddha, the Bearer of Truth, the Supremely Enlightened One!

May all beings be happy!

Venerable Acharya Buddharakkhita

Buddha Vachana Trust,
Mahā Bodhi Society,
Bangalore,
India, 2004.

# A Word to the Reader

Reading a book is both profitable and entertaining. Yet, it is quite seldom that such a good book comes our way. This occasional blessing can be said to have come to us through this book titled "Mind Overcoming its Cankers" authored by Venerable Acharya Buddharakkhita Thera of Banglore, India.

Readers are aware that there are many varieties of books such as novels, literary critisisms, books on travel, on sociology and so on. But, books on practical ethics are not so common. This is such an uncommon book worthy to be read and re-read because it is bound to help any deep-thinking person to improve oneself in one's day to day living style.

By reading it any person wishing his own welfare honestly (*attha-kusala*), can profit immensely from it because it silently prompts the reader to rid oneself of one's common weaknesses.

Moreover, although the author discusses Buddhism basing himself on a discourse delivered by the Buddha, any person, be he Buddhist or non-Buddhist, would find the guidance it provides helping one to drop at least some of one's more common shortcomings.

By any standard this is a Good Book. We wish our readers would profit from it.

A.G.S. Kariyawasam
(Editor, BPS)

# Introduction

By writing this book, Venerable Ācarya Buddharakkhita has made a significant contribution to the field of both Buddhology and psychology. Its relevance, however, is not limited to scholars, for it proves an admirable guide for all sincere seekers of truth.

As enunciated by the Buddha, the *āsavas* are those inherent mental cankers or pollutants with which we all are afflicted. These existential ulcers affect the fabric of all thought and action, both individual and societal. Until extirpated, they ensure the continued unsatisfactoriness of lives to come.

The three cankers are the canker of sensual desire, the canker of desire for continued existence, and the canker of ignorance. However, the simplicity of these categories belies their manifold and subtle ramifications. The path from diagnosis to deliverance leads one through the vast and intricate machinations of the human mind, from dormant tendency through thought, overt action, reaction and future *kamma*. The *āsavas* and the various approaches and techniques for their riddance, which form the subject of this treatise, have been propounded by the Enlightened One in specific, practical terms.

The Buddhologist will appreciate the thoroughgoing and painstaking care with which the author has collated hitherto scattered material from various sources, to present for the first time this comprehensive and incisive commentary. In addition to his own comments, he has presented the material as enunciated in the *Sabbāsava Sutta* and the *Nibbedhika Sutta*, along with the classic commentary of Ācariya Buddhaghosa. In lucid, concrete language he has also incorporated pertinent Buddhist stories and observations from his own rich background and wisdom.

The subject is then approached from the *Abhidhamma* point of view, in pure philosophical and scientific terms of analysis. The basis of this facet of the presentation is the *Dhammasaṅgaṇī*, the first book of the *Abhidhamma Piṭaka*. Here the *āsavas* have been expounded in two distinct ways as the *nikkhepa-kāṇḍa* treatment based on semantic analysis, and the *atthuddhāra-kāṇḍa* method, a condensed psychological analysis of the states of consciousness.

Let it not be assumed that one must be a Buddhist scholar to be able to understand and benefit from this work. Psychologists in particular will find their eyes opening in a new way. Ancient as it is, Buddhist psychology is far more refined than modern psychology, which in comparison resembles rough ore. Buddhism recognizes and is familiar with more levels of consciousness, and hence is more sophisticated. While subtle, it is not the subtleness of the nebulous, esoteric, fuzzy thinking commonly indulged in by dabblers in Eastern thought. It is, rather, the subtlety of the surgeon's scalpel, which precisely and incisively exposes the multidimensional workings of the complex aggregate known as the 'human mind'.

The achievements of Buddhist psychology are made possible by the underlying acceptance of the life process as the continuous flux of interaction between ever-changing subjective and objective phenomena. Boxed in by static metaphysical concepts, other schools and systems, no matter how "modern," cannot help but be limited. Hence the modern psychologist will find ample food for thought in the ideas herein presented. Along with the wreckage of some of his most cherished preconceptions, he will find that many of his exciting "new" ideas have existed for thousands of years as working principles, not mere theories. More important, he will find himself expanding his horizons as he questions his most basic premises and discovers unsuspected intricacies of the human consciousness.

The rich and varied texture of Buddhist psychology never obscures the simple, strong warp threads of the fundamental pattern of motivation and behaviour. The applied psychologist may find that his tools are too specialized and over-sophisticated for maximum effectiveness. For him this book can be the lost path back to the simple yet profound basics of human motivation, diagnosis and appropriate course correction. Meditation becomes a vital aspect of what is essentially a holistic approach to individual development.

Above all, this book is concerned with values and human potential. It is, therefore, a treasure trove for those concerned with improving the quality of life, discovering the upper ranges of man's capacity for fulfilment and furthering their spiritual evolution. Venerable Ācariya Buddharakkhita is not afraid to use the term "excellence" with regard to human aspirations and he does so with compelling force. Under the unique light that he provides, the reader will find himself turning inward to examine himself with ruthless honesty. And there, unless he is an enlightened saint, he will discover his cankers and their ulcerous ravages.

Buddhism is, above all, a practical approach to the development of excellence. Once the *āsavas* are acknowledged and recognized, they can be destroyed by the various specific methods as outlined by the Buddha and offered in these pages. In working towards the destruction of these insidious enemies, the reader will not only improve the quality and happiness of this life-time, but will be assured of continuing spiritual evolution in lives to come as well. With their ultimate destruction, he will be delivered from the bondage of phenomenal existence and be able to enter the Deathless state of Nibbāna.

**—Venerable Sīlamātā Karuṇā**

# Chapter 1

## *Sabbāsava Sutta*[1]

*Evaṃ me sutaṃ. Ekaṃ samayaṃ Bhagavā Sāvatthiyaṃ viharati Jetavane Anāthapiṇḍikassa ārāme. Tatra kho Bhagavā bhikkhū āmantesi: "Bhikkhavo'ti. "Bhadante'ti te bhikkhū Bhagavato paccassosuṃ. Bhagavā etadavoca: "Sabbāsava saṃvara-pariyāyaṃ vo bhikkhave desessāmi. Taṃ suṇātha, sādhukaṃ manasi karotha, bhāsissāmī'ti. "Evaṃ, bhante'ti kho te bhikkhū Bhagavato paccassosuṃ. Bhagavā etadavoca:*

*"Jānato ahaṃ bhikkhave, passato āsavānaṃ khayaṃ vadāmi, no ajānato no apassato. Kiñca bhikkhave, jānato kiñca passato āsavānaṃ khayaṃ vadāmi? Yoniso ca manasikāraṃ ayoniso ca manasikāraṃ. Ayoniso bhikkhave, manasikāroto anuppannā ceva āsavā uppajjanti, uppannā ca āsavā pavaḍḍhanti; yoniso ca kho bhikkhave, manasikaroto anup-pannā ceva āsavā na uppajjanti, uppannā ca āsavā pahīyanti.*

*"Atthi bhikkhave, āsavā dassanā pahātabbā, atthi āsavā saṃvarā pahātabbā, atthi āsavā paṭisevanā pahātabbā, atthi āsavā adhivāsanā pahātabbā, atthi āsavā parivajjanā pahātabbā, atthi āsavā vinodanā pahātabbā, atthi āsavā bhāvanā pahātabbā."*

### 1. *Dassanā pahātabbāsavā*

*"Katame ca bhikkhave, āsavā dassanā pahātabbā? Idha bhikkhave, assutavā puthujjano–ariyānaṃ adassāvī, ariya-dhammassa akovido, ariyadhamme avinīto, sappurisānaṃ*

1. Majjhima N. Sutta No. 02

*adassāvī, sappurisadhammassa akovido, sappurisadhamme avinīto–manasikaraṇīye dhamme nappajānāti, amanasikaraṇīye dhamme nappajānāti. So manasikaraṇīye dhamme appajānanto amanasikaraṇīye dhamme appajānanto ye dhammā na manasikaraṇīyā, te dhamme manasikaroti, ye dhammā manasikaraṇīyā te dhamme na manasikaroti.*

*"Katame ca bhikkhave, dhammā na manasikaraṇīyā ye dhamme manasikaroti? Yassa bhikkhave, dhamme manasikaroto anuppanno vā kāmāsavo uppajjati, uppanno vā kāmāsavo pavaḍḍhati; anuppanno vā bhavāsavo uppajjati, uppanno vā bhavāsavo pavaḍḍhati; anuppanno vā avijjāsavo uppajjati, uppanno vā avijjāsavo pavaḍḍhati–ime dhammā na manasikaraṇīyā ye dhamme manasikaroti.*

*"Katame ca bhikkhave, dhammā manasikaraṇīyā ye dhamme na manasikaroti? Yassa bhikkhave, dhamme manasikaroto anuppanno vā kāmāsavo na uppajjati, uppanno vā kāmāsavo pahīyati; anuppanno vā bhavāsavo na uppajjati, uppanno vā bhavāsavo pahīyati; anuppanno vā avijjāsavo na uppajjati, uppanno vā avijjāsavo pahīyati–ime dhammā manasikaraṇīyā ye dhamme na manasikaroti.*

*"Tassa amanasikaraṇīyānaṃ dhammānaṃ manasikārā manasikaraṇīyānaṃ dhammānaṃ amanasikārā anuppannā ceva āsavā uppajjanti uppannā ca āsavā pavaḍḍhanti.*

*"So evaṃ ayoniso manasikaroti: 'Ahosiṃ nu kho ahaṃ atītamaddhānaṃ? Na nu kho ahosiṃ atītamaddhānaṃ? Kiṃ nu kho ahosiṃ atītamaddhānaṃ? Kathaṃ nu kho ahosiṃ atītamaddhānaṃ? Kiṃ hutvā kiṃ ahosiṃ nu kho ahaṃ atītamaddhānaṃ? Bhavissāmi nu kho ahaṃ anāgatamaddhānaṃ? Na nu kho bhavissāmi anāgatamad dhānaṃ? Kiṃ nu kho bhavissāmi anāgatamaddhānaṃ? Kathaṃ nu kho bhavissāmi anāgatamaddhānaṃ? Kiṃ hutvā kiṃ bhavissāmi nu kho ahaṃ anāgatamaddhānan'ti? Etarahi vā paccuppannamaddhānaṃ ajjhattaṃ kathaṃkathī hoti: 'Ahaṃ nu khosmi? No nu khosmi? Kiṃ nu khosmi? Kathaṃ nu khosmi? Ayaṃ nu kho satto kuto āgato? So kuhiṃ gāmī bhavissatī'ti?*

*"Tassa evaṃ ayoniso manasikaroto channaṃ diṭṭhīnaṃ aññatarā diṭṭhi uppajjati. 'Atthi me attā' ti vā assa saccato thetato diṭṭhi uppajjati. 'Natthi me attā' ti vā assa saccato thetato diṭṭhi uppajjati. 'Attanāva attānaṃ sañjānāmī' ti vā assa saccato thetato diṭṭhi uppajjati. 'Attanāva anattānaṃ sañjānāmī' ti vā assa saccato thetato diṭṭhi uppajjati; 'anattanāva attānaṃ sañjānāmī' ti vā assa saccato thetato diṭṭhi uppajjati. Atha vā panassa evaṃ diṭṭhi hoti: 'Yo me ayaṃ attā vado vedeyyo tatra tatra kalyāṇapāpakānaṃ kammānaṃ vipākaṃ paṭisaṃvedeti so kho pana me ayaṃ attā nicco dhuvo sassato avipariṇāmadhammo sassatisamaṃ tatheva ṭhassatī 'ti. Idaṃ vuccati, bhikkhave, diṭṭhigataṃ diṭṭhigahanaṃ diṭṭhikantāraṃ diṭṭhivisūkaṃ diṭṭhivipphanditaṃ diṭṭhisaṃyojanaṃ. Diṭṭhisaṃyojanasaṃyutto, bhikkhave, assutavā puthujjano na parimuccati jātiyā jarāya maraṇena sokehi paridevehi dukkhehi domanassehi upāyāsehi; na parimuccati dukkhasmā' ti vadāmi.*

*"Sutavā ca kho bhikkhave, ariyasāvako–ariyānaṃ dassāvī ariyadhammassa kovido ariyadhamme suvinīto, sappurisānaṃ dassāvī sappurisa-dhammassa kovido sappurisa-dhamme suvinīto– manasikaraṇīye dhamme pajānāti amanasikaraṇīye dhamme pajānāti. So manasikaraṇīye dhamme pajānanto amanasikaraṇīye dhamme pajānanto ye dhammā na manasikaraṇīyā te dhamme na manasikaroti, ye dhammā manasikaraṇīyā te dhamme manasi karoti.*

*"Katame ca bhikkhave, dhammā na manasikaraṇīyā ye dhamme na manasi karoti? Yassa bhikkhave, dhamme manasikaroto anuppanno vā kāmāsavo uppajjati, uppanno vā kāmāsavo pavaḍḍhati; anuppanno vā bhavāsavo uppajjati, uppanno vā bhavāsavo pavaḍḍhati; anuppanno vā avijjāsavo uppajjati, uppanno vā avijjāsavo pavaḍḍhati–ime dhammā na manasikaraṇīyā, ye dhamme na manasikaroti.*

*"Katame ca bhikkhave, dhammā manasikaraṇīyā ye dhamme manasikaroti? Yassa, bhikkhave, dhamme manasikaroto anuppanno vā kāmāsavo na uppajjati, uppanno vā kāmāsavo pahīyati; anuppanno vā bhavāsavo na uppajjati,*

*uppanno vā bhavāsavo pahīyati; anuppanno vā avijjāsavo na uppajjati, uppanno vā avijjāsavo pahīyati–ime dhammā manasikaraṇīyā ye dhamme manasikaroti.*

*"Tassa amanasikaraṇīyānaṃ dhammānaṃ amanasikārā manasikaraṇīyānaṃ dhammānaṃ manasikārā anuppannā ceva āsavā na uppajjanti, uppannā ca āsavā pahīyanti.*

*"So 'Idaṃ dukkhan'ti yoniso manasikaroti, 'Ayaṃ dukkhasamudayo'ti yoniso manasikaroti, 'Ayaṃ dukkhanirodho'ti yoniso manasikaroti, 'Ayaṃ dukkhanirodhagāminīpaṭipa-dā'ti yoniso manasi karoti. Tassa evaṃ yoniso manasikaroto tīṇi saṃyojanāni pahīyanti–sakkāyadiṭṭhi, vicikicchā, sīlabbataparāmāso. Ime vuccanti bhikkhave, āsavā dassanā pahātabbā."*

## 2. *Saṃvarā pahātabbāsavā*

*"Katame ca bhikkhave, āsavā saṃvarā pahātabbā? Idha bhikkhave, bhikkhu paṭisaṅkhā yoniso cakkhundriyasaṃvarasaṃvuto viharati. Yañhissa, bhikkhave, cakkhundriyasaṃvaraṃ asaṃvutassa viharato uppajjeyyuṃ āsavā vighātapariḷāhā, cakkhundriyasaṃvaraṃ saṃvutassa viharato evaṃsa te āsavā vighātapariḷāhā na honti.*

*Idha bhikkhave, bhikkhu paṭisaṅkhā yoniso sotindriyasaṃvarasaṃvuto viharati. Yañhissa bhikkhave, soti-ndriyasaṃvaraṃ asaṃvutassa viharato uppajjeyyuṃ āsavā vighātapariḷāhā, sotindriyasaṃvaraṃ saṃvutassa viharato evaṃsa te āsavā vighātapariḷāhā na honti.*

*Idha bhikkhave, bhikkhu paṭisaṅkhā yoniso ghānindriyasaṃvarasaṃvuto viharati. Yañhissa, bhikkhave, ghānindriyasaṃvaraṃ asaṃvutassa viharato uppajjeyyuṃ āsavā vighātapariḷāhā, ghānindriyasaṃvaraṃ saṃvutassa viharato evaṃsa te āsavā vighātapariḷāhā na honti.*

*Idha bhikkhave, bhikkhu paṭisaṅkhā yoniso jivhindriyasaṃvarasaṃvuto viharati. Yañhissa, bhikkhave, jivhindriyasaṃvaraṃ asaṃvutassa viharato uppajjeyyuṃ āsavā vighātapariḷāhā, jivhindriyasaṃvaraṃ saṃvutassa viharato evaṃsa te āsavā vighātapariḷāhā na honti.*

*Idha bhikkhave, bhikkhu paṭisaṅkhā yoniso kāyindriyasaṃvarasaṃvuto viharati. Yañhissa, bhikkhave, kāyindriyasaṃvaraṃ asaṃvutassa viharato uppajjeyyuṃ āsavā vighātapariḷāhā, kāyindriyasaṃvaraṃ saṃvutassa viharato evaṃsa te āsavā vighātapariḷāhā na honti.*

*Idha bhikkhave, bhikkhu paṭisaṅkhā yoniso manindriyasaṃvarasaṃvuto viharati. Yañhissa bhikkhave, manindriyasaṃvaraṃ asaṃvutassa viharato uppajjeyyuṃ āsavā vighātapariḷāhā, manindriyasaṃvaraṃ saṃvutassa viharato evaṃsa te āsavā vighātapariḷāhā na honti.*

*"Yañhissa bhikkhave, saṃvaraṃ asaṃvutassa viharato uppajjeyyuṃ āsavā vighātapariḷāhā, saṃvaraṃ saṃvutassa viharato evaṃsa te āsavā vighātapariḷāhā na honti. Ime vuccanti, bhikkhave, āsavā saṃvarā pahātabbā."*

### 3. *Paṭisevanā pahātabbāsavā*

*"Katame ca bhikkhave, āsavā paṭisevanā pahātabbā? Idha, bhikkhave, bhikkhu paṭisaṅkhā yoniso cīvaraṃ paṭisevati: 'Yāvadeva sītassa paṭighātāya, uṇhassa paṭighātāya, ḍaṃsamakasavātātapa-sarīṃsapasamphassānaṃ paṭighātāya, yāvadeva hirikopīnappaṭicchādanatthaṃ '."*

*"Paṭisaṅkhā yoniso piṇḍapātaṃ paṭisevati: 'Neva davāya, na madāya, na maṇḍanāya, na vibhūsanāya, yāvadeva imassa kāyassa ṭhitiyā, yāpanāya, vihiṃsūparatiyā, brahmacariyānuggahāya, iti purāṇañca vedanaṃ paṭihaṅkhāmi navañca vedanaṃ na uppādessāmi, yātrā ca me bhavissati anavajjatā ca phāsuvihāro ca'.*

*"Paṭisaṅkhā yoniso senāsanaṃ paṭisevati: 'Yāvadeva sītassa paṭighātāya, uṇhassa paṭighātāya, ḍaṃsamakasavātātapasarīṃsapasamphassānaṃ paṭighātāya, yāvadeva utuparissayavinodanapaṭisallānārāmatthaṃ '."*

*"Paṭisaṅkhā yoniso gilānappaccaya-bhesajjaparikkhāraṃ paṭisevati: 'Yāvadeva uppannānaṃ veyyābādhikānaṃ vedanānaṃ paṭighātāya, abyābajjhaparamatāya?.*

*"Yañhissa bhikkhave, appaṭisevato uppajjeyyuṃ āsavā vighātapariḷāhā, paṭisevato evaṃsa te āsavā vighātapariḷāhā na honti. Ime vuccanti bhikkhave, āsavā paṭisevanā pahātabbā."*

**4. *Adhivāsanā pahātabbāsavā***

*"Katame ca bhikkhave, āsavā adhivāsanā pahātabbā? Idha, bhikkhave, bhikkhu paṭisaṅkhā yoniso khamo hoti sītassa uṇhassa, jighacchāya pipāsāya. Ḍaṃsa-makasa-vātātapa-sarīṃsapasamphassānaṃ, duruttānaṃ durāgatānaṃ vacana-pathānaṃ, uppannānaṃ sārīrikānaṃ vedanānaṃ dukkhānaṃ tibbānaṃ kharānaṃ kaṭukānaṃ asātānaṃ amanāpānaṃ pāṇaharānaṃ adhivāsakajātiko hoti.*

*"Yañhissa bhikkhave, anadhivāsayato uppajjeyyuṃ āsavā vighātapariḷāhā, adhivāsayato evaṃsa te āsavā vighātapariḷāhā na honti. Ime vuccanti, bhikkhave, āsavā adhivāsanā pahātabbā."*

**5. *Parivajjanā pahātabbāsavā***

*"Katame ca bhikkhave, āsavā parivajjanā pahātabbā? Idha bhikkhave, bhikkhu paṭisaṅkhā yoniso caṇḍaṃ hatthiṃ parivajjeti, caṇḍaṃ assaṃ parivajjeti, caṇḍaṃ goṇaṃ parivajjeti, caṇḍaṃ kukkuraṃ parivajjeti, ahiṃ khāṇuṃ kaṇṭakaṭṭhānaṃ sobbhaṃ papātaṃ candanikaṃ oḷigallaṃ. Yathārūpe anāsane nisinnaṃ yathārūpe agocare carantaṃ yathārūpe pāpake mitte bhajantaṃ viññū sabrahmacārī pāpakesu ṭhānesu okappeyyuṃ, so tañca anāsanaṃ tañca agocaraṃ te ca pāpake mitte paṭisaṅkhā yoniso parivajjeti.*

*"Yañhissa bhikkhave, aparivajjayato uppajjeyyuṃ āsavā vighātapariḷāhā, parivajjayato evaṃsa te āsavā vighātapariḷāhā na honti. Ime vuccanti bhikkhave, āsavā parivajjanā pahātabbā."*

**6. *Vinodanā pahātabbāsavā***

*"Katame ca bhikkhave, āsavā vinodanā pahātabbā? Idha bhikkhave, bhikkhu paṭisaṅkhā yoniso uppannaṃ kāmavitakkaṃ nādhivāseti pajahati vinodeti byantīkaroti anabhāvaṃ gameti, uppannaṃ byāpādavitakkaṃ nādhivāseti pajahati vinodeti byantīkaroti anabhāvaṃ gameti, uppannaṃ vihiṃsāvitakkaṃ nādhivāseti pajahati vinodeti byantīkaroti anabhāvaṃ gameti, uppannuppanne pāpake akusale dhamme nādhivāseti pajahati vinodeti byantīkaroti anabhāvaṃ gameti.*

*"Yañhissa bhikkhave, avinodayato uppajjeyyuṃ āsavā vighātapariḷāhā, vinodayato evaṃsa te āsavā vighātapariḷāhā na honti. Ime vuccanti bhikkhave, āsavā vinodanā pahātabbā."*

**7. *Bhāvanā pahātabbāsavā***

*"Katame ca bhikkhave, āsavā bhāvanā pahātabbā? Idha bhikkhave, bhikkhu paṭisaṅkhā yoniso satisambojjhaṅgaṃ bhāveti vivekanissitaṃ virāganissitaṃ nirodhanissitaṃ vossaggapariṇāmiṃ; paṭisaṅkhā yoniso dhammavicayasambojjhaṅgaṃ bhāveti vivekanissitaṃ virāganissitaṃ nirodhanissitaṃ vossaggapariṇāmiṃ; paṭisaṅkhā yoniso vīriyasambojjhaṅgaṃ bhāveti vivekanissitaṃ virāganissitaṃ nirodhanissitaṃ vossagga-pariṇāmiṃ; paṭisaṅkhā yoniso pītisambojjhaṅgaṃ bhāveti passaddhisambojjhaṅgaṃ bhāveti vivekanissitaṃ virāganissitaṃ nirodhanissitaṃ vossaggapariṇāmiṃ; paṭisaṅkhā yoniso samādhisambojjhaṅgaṃ bhāveti vivekanissitaṃ virāganissitaṃ nirodhanissitaṃ vossaggapariṇāmiṃ; paṭisaṅkhā yoniso upekkhāsambojjhaṅgaṃ bhāveti viveka-nissitaṃ virāganissitaṃ nirodhanissitaṃ vossaggapariṇāmiṃ.*

*"Yañhissa, bhikkhave, abhāvayato uppajjeyyuṃ āsavā vighātapariḷāhā, bhāvayato evaṃsa te āsavā vighātapariḷāhā na honti. Ime vuccanti, bhikkhave, āsavā bhāvanā pahātabbā.*

*"Yato kho bhikkhave, bhikkhuno ye āsavā dassanā pahātabbā te dassanā pahīnā honti, ye āsavā saṃvarā pahātabbā te saṃvarā pahīnā honti, ye āsavā paṭisevanā pahātabbā te*

*paṭisevanā pahīnā honti, ye āsavā adhivāsanā pahātabbā te adhivāsanā pahīnā honti, ye āsavā parivajjanā pahātabbā te parivajjanā pahīnā honti, ye āsavā vinodanā pahātabbā te vinodanā pahīnā honti, ye āsavā bhāvanā pahātabbā te bhāvanā pahīnā honti; ayaṃ vuccati bhikkhave: 'Bhikkhu sabbāsava-saṃvarasaṃvuto viharati, acchecchi taṇhaṃ, vivattayi saṃyojanaṃ, sammā mānābhisamayā antamakāsi dukkhassā'ti."*

*Idamavoca Bhagavā. Attamanā te bhikkhū Bhagavato bhāsitaṃ abhinandunti.*

# Chapter 2

## Discourse On All-Cankers[1]

Thus have I heard:
Once the Blessed One was staying at the monastery of Anāthapiṇḍika in the Jeta's Grove near Sāvatthi. There the Blessed One addressed the monks, saying 'Monks!' 'Most Venerable Sir,' the monks replied to the Blessed One. The Blessed One said: "Monks, I shall now expound to you the method of controlling all cankers. Listen and consider carefully. I shall now enunciate." "Yes, Most Venerable Sir," the monks replied to the Blessed One. And the Blessed One spoke thus:

"Only for him who understands, who comprehends, is there the destruction of cankers, so I say; not for him who does not understand, who does not comprehend. And, monks, understanding what, comprehending what, is there the destruction of cankers, do I say? There is the wise consideration and there is the unwise consideration. Monks, for one who unwisely considers, the unarisen cankers arise, and the arisen cankers increase; and, monks, for one who wisely considers, the unarisen cankers do not arise and the arisen cankers are overcome."

"Monks, there are cankers to be overcome by Insight.
There are cankers to be overcome by Self-control.
There are cankers to be overcome by Judicious Use.
There are cankers to be overcome by Endurance.
There are cankers to be overcome by Avoidance.

1. From Sutta Sangaho-Selected Discourses of the Buddha, Part II, translated into English by Venerable Acharya Buddharakkhita, Buddha Vacana Trust, Maha Bodhi Society, Bangalore.

There are cankers to be overcome by Elimination.
There are cankers to be overcome by Development."

## 1. Cankers to be overcome by Insight

"And what monks, are the cankers to be overcome by Insight? Here, monks, an uninstructed ordinary person[1] - one who does not pay respect (lit.see) to the noble ones, who is unconversant with the Teachings of the noble ones, who is uninitiated in the Teachings of the noble ones; one who does not pay respect to the holy ones, who is unconversant with the teachings of the holy ones, who is uninitiated in the teachings of the holy ones - does not understand things which should be considered, does not understand things which should not be considered. Not understanding things to be considered, not understanding things not to be considered, he considers those things which should not be considered, and does not consider those things which should be considered.

"And what monks, are the things which should not be considered, but which he considers? Monks, things regarding which, while considering, the unarisen canker of sensual desire arises, or the already arisen canker of sensual desire increases; or the unarisen canker of the continuation of becoming arises, or the arisen canker of the continuation of becoming increases; or the unarisen canker of ignorance arises, or the arisen canker of ignorance increases—these are the things which should not be considered, but which he considers."

"And what monks, are the things which should be

1. A worldling (*puthujjana*) means one who is still fettered to the Wheel of Becoming, who has not yet outgrown the world, one very much caught in the net of kamma and rebirth. The term 'worldling' is the opposite of "Ariya", the Noble One, who is spiritually transformed. There are four types of Ariyas namely, the Stream-enterer (*Sotāpanna*), the Once-returner (*Sakadāgāmin*), the Non-returner (*anāgāmin*), the Accomplished One (Arahat). These designations refer to the progress these saints have made by way of abandoning the fetters and thereby the planes of existence. There are two kinds of worldlings—one who is deeply involved in the world, and the other, known as kalyāṇa-puthujjana, a sincere one who is trying to outgrow the bondage of the world.

considered, but which he does not consider? Monks, things regarding which, while considering, the unarisen canker of sensual desire does not arise, or the arisen canker of sensual desire is overcome; or the unarisen canker of the continuation of becoming does not arise, or the arisen canker of the continuation of becoming is overcome; or the unarisen canker of ignorance does not arise, or the arisen canker of ignorance is overcome. These are the things that should be considered which he does not consider.

"By considering things which should not be considered, and by not considering things which should be considered, his unarisen cankers arise and the arisen cankers increase.

"Thus he unwisely considers: – 'Was I in the past? Or was I not in the past? Or what was I in the past? Or how was I in the past? Or what having been, what then was I in the past? Will I be in the future? Or will I not be in the future? Or what will I be in the future? Or how will I be in the future? Or what having been, what then will I be in the future?' He also becomes inwardly perplexed with reference to the present, thinking: 'Indeed am I? Or am I not? Or what am I? Or how am I? Or whence has this 'being' come? Or where will it be going'?

"While unwisely considering thus, any one of these six wrong views arises in him: 'There is self in me', this wrong view arises in him as being true and real; or 'There is no self in me', this wrong view arises in him as being true and real; or 'By myself alone do I know the self', this wrong view arises in him as being true and real; or 'By myself alone do I know the non-self,' this wrong view arises in him as being true and real; or 'By my non-self alone do I know the self' this wrong view arises in him as being true and real; or again, the wrong view arises in him thus: 'Whatever this self is in me, that speaks, that feels, that experiences, now here, now there, the result of the good and evil deeds, indeed, it is this self in me that is permanent, stable, eternal, beyond the scope of changefulness, and that will last as eternity itself.'

"Monks, this is called the hold of wrong views, the thicket of wrong views, the wilderness of wrong views, the wriggling of wrong views, the writhing of wrong views and the fetter of wrong views. Monks, fettered by the fetter of wrong views, the uninstructed ordinary person is not freed from birth, from ageing, from death, from sorrowing, from lamenting, from pain, from depression, from despair; indeed, he is not freed from suffering, so I declare.

"But, monks, the well-instructed noble disciple—one who pays respect to the noble ones, who is fully conversant with the teachings of the noble ones, who is an adept in the teachings of the noble ones, one who pays respect to the holy ones, who is fully conversant with the teachings of the holy ones, who is an adept in the teachings of the holy ones,—understands things which should be considered, understands things which should not be considered. Understanding things which should be considered and understanding things which should not be considered, he does not consider those things which should not be considered, and considers those things which should be considered.

"And what, monks, are the things that should not be considered which he does not consider? Monks, things regarding which, while considering, the unarisen canker of sensual desire arises, or the already arisen canker of sensual desire increases; or the unarisen canker of the continuation of becoming arises, or the arisen canker of the continuation of becoming increases; or the unarisen canker of ignorance arises, or the arisen canker of ignorance increases—these are the things that should not be considered, which he does not consider.

"And what, monks, are the things which should be considered, and which he considers? Monks, things regarding which, while considering, the unarisen canker of sensual desire does not arise or the arisen canker of sensual desire is overcome; or the unarisen canker of the continuation of becoming does not arise, or the arisen canker of the continuation of becoming is overcome; or the unarisen canker of ignorance does not arise, or the arisen canker of ignorance is overcome; —these are the things which should be considered, and which he considers.

"By not considering things which should not be considered, and by considering things which should be considered, his unarisen cankers do not arise and the arisen cankers are overcome.

"This is suffering", so he wisely considers. 'This is the cause of suffering', so he wisely considers. 'This is the cessation of suffering' so he wisely considers. 'This is the path leading to the cessation of suffering,' so he wisely considers. While thus wisely considering, his three fetters are overcome, *viz.* self-illusion, doubt, clinging to rules and rituals. Monks, these are called the cankers to be overcome by (supramundane) insight."

## 2. Overcoming cankers by self-control

"Monks, what are the cankers to be overcome by self-control? Monks, here a monk, wisely reflecting, lives self-controlled, by having control over the sense-organ of the eye. Monks, whatever destructive and consuming cankers might arise by living uncontrolled, by not having control over the sense-organ of the eye, now, by living self-controlled, by having control over the sense-organ of the eye, these cankers do not become destructive and consuming.

"Monks, here a monk, wisely reflecting, lives self-controlled, by having control over the sense-organ of the ear. Monks, whatever destructive and consuming cankers might arise by living uncontrolled, by not having control over the sense-organ of the ear, now, by living self-controlled, by having control over the sense-organ of the ear, these cankers do not become destructive and consuming.

"Monks, here a monk, wisely reflecting, lives self-controlled, by having control over the sense-organ of the nose. Monks, whatever destructive and consuming cankers might arise by living uncontrolled, by not having control over the sense-organ of the nose, now, by living self-controlled, by having control over the sense-organ of the nose, these cankers do not become destructive and consuming.

"Monks, here a monk, wisely reflecting, lives self-controlled, by having control over the sense-organ of the tongue. Monks, whatever destructive and consuming cankers might arise by living uncontrolled, by not having control over the sense-organ of the tongue, now, by living self-controlled, by having control over the sense-organ of the tongue, these cankers do not become destructive and consuming.

"Monks, here a monk, wisely reflecting, lives self-controlled, by having control over the sense-organ of the body. Monks, whatever destructive and consuming cankers might arise by living uncontrolled, by not having control over the sense-organ of the body, now, by living self-controlled, by having control over the sense-organ of the body, these cankers do not become destructive and consuming.

"Monks, here a monk, wisely reflecting, lives self-controlled, by having control over the mental-organ of the mind. Monks, whatever destructive and consuming cankers might arise by living uncontrolled, by not having control over the mental-organ of the mind, now, by living self-controlled, by having control over the mental-organ of the mind, these cankers do not become destructive and consuming.

"Monks, whatever destructive and consuming cankers might arise by living uncontrolled, by not having control (over the sense and mind), now, by living self-controlled, by having control (over the sense and mind), these cankers do not become destructive and consuming. Monks, these are called the cankers to be overcome by self-control."

### 3. Cankers to be overcome by judicious use

"Monks, what are the cankers to be overcome by judicious use? Monks, here a monk, wisely reflecting, uses the robe simply for warding off cold, warding off heat, warding off gadfly, mosquito, wind, sun-burn and the contact of creeping creatures, and only for the sake of covering nakedness.

"Wisely reflecting, he uses the alms-food, not for fun, not for indulgence, nor for show, not for good looks, but only for the sake of supporting and sustaining this body, for keeping it out of harm, and for upholding the holy life, thinking: 'In this way do I get rid of the already existing feeling (of hunger), and will not allow the arising of a new feeling of pain (through over-eating), so that it will conduce to my longevity and (a life of) blamelessness and comfort.

"Wisely reflecting, he uses the dwelling simply for warding off cold, warding off heat, warding off gadfly, mosquito, wind, sun-burn and the contact of creeping creatures, and only for the sake of dispelling the discomforts of the seasons as well as to delight in seclusion.

"Wisely reflecting, he uses the requisite of medicaments for health care, only for the sake of warding off uncomfortable feelings that have arisen, and for maximum well-being.

"Monks, whatever destructive and consuming cankers might arise through injudicious use, now, by making such judicious use, these cankers do not become destructive and consuming. Monks, these are called the cankers to be overcome by judicious use."

## 4. Cankers to be overcome by endurance

"Monks, what are the cankers to be overcome by endurance? Monks, here a monk, wisely reflecting, is an endurer of cold, heat, hunger and thirst. He is one who endures gadflies, mosquitoes, wind, sun-burn and the contact of creeping creatures, and such modes of speech that are harsh and unpleasant, and such bodily feelings, which arising, are painful, shooting, cutting, sharp, excruciating, miserable and life-threatening.

"Monks, whatever destructive and consuming cankers might

arise through non-endurance, now, by such endurance, these cankers do not become destructive and consuming. Monks, these are called the cankers to be overcome by endurance."

### 5. Cankers to be overcome by avoidance

"Monks, what are the cankers to be overcome by avoidance? Monks, here a monk, wisely reflecting, avoids a fierce elephant, horse or bull, a ferocious dog, a snake, a tree stump, a thorny brake, a deep hole, a precipice, a cesspool, a garbage pit. Wisely reflecting, he avoids sitting in such unbecoming seats, or resorting to such unbecoming resorts, or associating with such depraved friends, because of which his wise fellow-monks in the holy life would suspect him of depraved conduct.

"Monks, whatever destructive and consuming cankers might arise through non-avoidance, now, by such avoidance, these cankers do not become destructive and consuming. Monks, these are called the cankers to be overcome by avoidance."

### 6. Cankers to be overcome by elimination

"Monks, what, are the cankers to be overcome by elimination? Monks, here a monk, wisely reflecting, does not tolerate an arisen thought of sensuality; he gets rid of it, makes an end of it, liquidates it. He does not tolerate an arisen thought of ill-will; he gets rid of it, eliminates it, makes an end of it, and liquidates it. He does not tolerate an arisen thought of cruelty; he gets rid of it, eliminates it, makes an end of it, and liquidates it. He does not tolerate any evil and unwholesome mental conditions; whenever they may arise, he gets rid of them, eliminates them, makes and end of them and liquidates them.

"Monks, whatever destructive and consuming cankers might arise by non-elimination, now, by such elimination, these cankers do not become destructive and consuming. Monks, these are called the cankers to be overcome by elimination."

## 7. Cankers to be overcome by development

"Monks, what are the cankers to be overcome by development? Monks, here a monk, wisely reflecting, develops the enlightenment-factor of mindfulness, which is supported by detachment, dispassion and cessation, and which culminates in renunciation; wisely reflecting, he develops the enlightenment-factor of the investigation of truth, which is supported by detachment, dispassion and cessation, and which culminates in renunciation; wisely reflecting, he develops the enlightenment-factor of effort, which is supported by detachment, dispassion and cessation and which culminates in renunciation; wisely reflecting, he develops the enlightenment-factor of rapture, which is supported by detachment, dispassion and cessation, and which culminates in renunciation; wisely reflecting, he develops the enlightenment-factor of tranquillity, which is supported by detachment, dispassion and cessation and which culminates in renunciation; wisely reflecting, he develops the enlightenment-factor of meditative concentration, which is supported by detachment, dispassion and cessation and which culminates in renunciation; wisely reflecting, he develops the enlightenment-factor of equanimity, which is supported by detachment, dispassion and cessation, and which culminates in renunciation.

"Monks, whatever destructive and consuming cankers might arise due to non-development, now, by such development, these cankers do not become destructive and consuming. Monks, these are called the cankers to be overcome by development."

*"In factors leading to Enlightenment*
*Whose minds have reached*
*The fullest excellence;*
*Who only delight in*
*Renouncing possessiveness and*
*In not clinging to things;*

*Having got rid of cankers*
*And glowing with wisdom*
*They have attained Nibbāna in this very life."*

-*Dhammapada*, 89

# Chapter 3

## EXEGESIS BASED ON COMMENTARY

The *Sabbāsava Sutta* was enunciated by the Buddha at Sāvatthi, while staying at Jeta's Grove in the monastery built by Anāthapiṇḍika. While commenting on the circumstances in which the *Sutta* was enunciated, Ācariya Buddhaghosa makes some very interesting observations. His remarks often tend to be quite extensive and are interesting in their own way in the context. For the purpose of this treatise, however, we shall stick only to certain pertinent points. For instance, commenting on the city of Sāvatthi, he says that (the name) Sāvatthi is so coined because it is a city which has everything in it—*sabbāni atthi iti Sāvatthi*—'Everything is found here'—hence the appellation 'All-found' (*Sāvatthi*). Similarly, remarking about Jeta and Anāthapiṇḍika, he questions, 'Why should their names appear in the body of the *Sutta* as if they need to be formally eulogised'? He answers it himself, saying that it is for the benefit of posterity: *puññakāmānaṃ diṭṭhānugati āpajjanatthāya*—'to inspire and to provide a "living example" to those who seek to perform acts of merit in times to come.'

Why did the Buddha give this discourse, saying: "Monks, I shall now expound to you the method of controlling of all cankers"? In order to effect the total destruction of cankers in those monks, by cleansing their minds of the slightest of impurities and establishing them on the path leading to the total destruction of cankers. Here, 'the method of controlling all cankers' means the technique which, by itself, acts to control and gets rid of all cankers. That is to say, the means by which the cankers are cleared and put away in a manner that they are destroyed, abandoned and never recur, as implied by terms such as extinguished, irreversible etc. What is indicated by a 'method of controlling' is an effective practical device.

"Here, canker (*āsava*) means whatever flows out. As it is said, it discharges, it oozes from the sense faculties; that is to say eye, ear, nose, tongue, body and the mind. In terms of internal phenomena, i.e. states of consciousness, it flows until it reaches the threshold state of the supramundane path-insight—the state of *gotrabhū.* And in terms of external phenomena, *i.e.* the various planes of existence, it flows to the very end of the cosmos. Therefore it is called "canker". The meaning is that it exudes all-inclusively by bringing these mental states, as well as these external cosmic dimensions, within its gamut. Thus, it is characterised by the quality of permeating everything.

"Alternatively, it is canker in the sense of something that has been fermenting for long, like liquor and such other spirits. Thus, because it is like a fermented stuff, it is 'canker.' In the world, fermented products such as vintage wine are considered alcoholic. In the same way, what is a long process of mental fermentation is a canker. It is in this context that the Buddha said: 'Monks, the first beginning of ignorance is inconceivable. No one can say that before this there was no ignorance.'(AN. X,61).

"Again, whatever extends or prolongs is also canker, in that it perpetuates the process of suffering in phenomenal existence. Of these definitions of canker, the first one stands for *āsava* as defilement, the second for *āsava* as *kamma*. Not only does canker connote defilement and *kamma*, but it also means varieties of distress or misfortune as implied by the last definition.

"In the discourses, the reference 'Cunda, I don't teach the

Dhamma only for the riddance of cankers pertaining to the life here and now'(D. III, 130)—implying something as the very root-cause of involvements or conflicts, stands for the cankers as defilements (*kilesa*)."

Or the reference:

'Those whereby one is born among the gods,
Or as a *gandhabba* or as a bird,
Or whereby one goes to the realm of the *yakkhas*,
Or one finds a birth amidst human beings,
Those cankers for me have been destroyed
Indeed they are demolished and annihilated.'

(AN. IV, 36).

"Here, *kamma* pertaining to the three realms of existence, as well as the unwholesome factors following thereof, are implied.

"Again the reference: 'for the purpose of ridding the cankers pertaining to life here and now and for the purpose of warding off the cankers pertaining to life hereafter" (Vin. III, 21) here, the various forms of misfortune, such as false accusations by others, or being guilty of crimes like murder, assault etc., or the innumerable oppressive forms of suffering as experienced in the various woe-ridden, fallen states of existence—these stand for *āsava* as 'misfortune.' Whatever is the connotation of 'canker,' what is meant in a given context has to be identified and understood in the proper perspective.

"With regard to the various classifications of cankers, the text as found in the *Vinaya*, 'for the purpose of ridding the cankers pertaining to life here and now, and for the purpose of warding off cankers pertaining to life hereafter' implies *āsavas* of two distinct types.

"Similarly, the text as found in the *Salāyatana Vagga*, 'there are these three types of cankers, bhikkhus: the canker of sensual desire, the canker of desire for the continuity of existence and the canker of ignorance' ( S. IV. 256) —implies three types.

"In several other *suttas* (discourses) as well as in the Abhidhamma, these three cankers, together with the canker of wrong view (*diṭṭhi*), constitute a four-fold classification.

"The text, as found in the *Nibbedha-pariyāya Sutta* (The Penetration Methodology), mentions this five-fold classification: 'Monks, there are cankers which lead one to the hells, there are cankers which lead one to the animal kingdom, there are cankers which lead one to the realm of the ghosts, there are cankers which lead one to the world of human beings and there are cankers which lead one to the divine sphere.' (AN. VI, 63).

"The text, as found in the *Chakka Nipāta* (*Aṅguttara Nikāya*): 'Monks, there are cankers to be overcome through self-restraint' and so on, provides a six-fold classification of *āsavas*' (*AN*. VI, 58).

"In this *sutta*, these six coupled with 'cankers to be overcome through insight', form a seven-fold classification. Thus are presented the definitions as well as the classifications of the term *āsava*, canker."

"Now, with regards to the term 'control', it means to get rid of cankers, that is to say, to overcome, to ward off and not allow them to arise. As it is said in these texts: 'I enjoin upon you monks to close the door of your rooms when you retire there to take rest" (*Vin*. III, 39), and, 'restraining currents of craving, do I exhort, with wisdom are they quelled.' (*Sn. stz*. 1041). In both of these texts, the term control is used in the sense of overcoming. This control (*saṃvara*) is of five kinds, namely, control by virtue, by mindfulness, by wisdom, by patience and by effort. There 'he abides by the code of monastic conduct' (*Vibh*. 246) implies control by virtue, for the monastic code of conduct as virtue is one form of control.

"Similarly 'one living self-controlled by having control over the sense-organs of the eye, ear, etc.' Here, control by mindfulness is meant. In other words mindfulness itself is a mode of control."

"Again,
'Restraining, do I exhort,
The currents of craving,
With wisdom alone
Are they quelled.' (*Sn.* 1041).

"This refers to control by wisdom. Since wisdom controls in the sense of quelling the currents, it has been referred to as a mode of control.

"Again, 'he is one who bears cold, heat, hunger and thirst,' etc., and 'he does not endure an arisen thought of sensuality, he gets rid of it,' (*MN.2)* etc. imply control by endurance and by effort respectively. All these five modes of control are indicated by the phrase 'The method of control of all cankers'. So it is to be understood.

"Of the five modes of control incorporated in the *Sabbāsava Sutta*, control by endurance and by effort have been already mentioned. Where it is said, 'wisely reflecting he avoids sitting in such unseemly seats, or resorting to such unseemly resorts' etc., there it refers to control by the monastic code of conduct. And, 'wisely reflecting, he lives self-controlled by having control over the sense-organ of the eye' etc. implies control by mindfulness. Wherever the expression 'wisely reflecting' occurs, it stands for control by wisdom and by this token the three methods, that is, overcoming by insight, by judicious use and by development, also stand for control by wisdom."

It is to be noted here that the seven methods of overcoming cankers, namely, by insight (into the Four Noble Truths), by self-control, by judicious use (of the essential needs like food etc.), by endurance, by avoidance (of wrong company, place etc.), by elimination (of wrong thoughts) and by development (of positive spiritual factors which form the central theme of the *Sabbāsava Sutta*), are anticipated by the five types of control already mentioned: that is to say, control by virtue, by wisdom, by mindfulness, by endurance and by effort. But these five modes of control cannot be really effective unless they are rooted in wise consideration. Wise consideration, therefore, constitutes the actual core and the operative tool of the entire technique.

That is why the emphasis is laid by the Buddha on the person "who understands, who comprehends" and not "who does not understand, who does not comprehend." However, virtuous and devout a person may be, however self-controlled and abstemious, unless he or she has insights into the working of the mind and into the basically conditioned nature of things, he or she just cannot uproot the cankers because they are so tenacious, subtle and insidious.

It is also to be borne clearly in mind that the term 'method' does not mean system, in the sense of a convenient arrangement conventionally evolved, nor is it a stratagem, a mere expedient to achieve a certain result. It is not a scheme for work, but a working psychological tool, a dynamic state of consciousness.

These two are important points, namely, that 'method' refers to the modes of control themselves, and that 'method' is not a static system or plan, but a dynamic operative principle. It is a mental reality, which, by virtue of its dynamism, is in flux—arises and passes away like any other phenomenon. These points have been made explicit by the commentator in the following passage, lest this unique and eminently practical technique is sought to be rendered into a mere theory by lesser minds.

"And by the term 'method', these five types of control are signified, which, like all phenomena, are also subject to arising and passing away. Therefore, it is to be understood that 'method' implies a dynamic inner state. Thus far, whatever has to be made explicit concerning the phrase, 'the method of control of all cankers' has now been made.

"With reference to 'only for him who understands, who comprehends, is there the destruction of cankers, so I say,' the terms 'understands' and 'comprehends' are synonyms. They mean the same thing though in different words. However, specifically, *i.e.,* in this context, 'one who understands' means 'one who is able to rouse wise consideration'. And 'one who comprehends' means 'one who comprehends in such a manner that unwise consideration may not arise.' Wise consideration is thus the underlying purpose."

With reference to the destruction of cankers, the commentary says that it is only the attainment of the supramundane path and fruition insights as well as the transcendental dimension of Nibbāna, which is an occasion of destruction in the sense of the *āsavas* being uprooted once and for all. This means that only the first and the last of the seven methods, comprising control by wisdom, can really be construed as causing the destruction of the cankers.

Why then are the five remaining methods enunciated, when they cannot uproot the cankers? Destruction of cankers, in this specific sense, implies two distinct accomplishments:

(i) An "uprooting", which annihilates the cankers, so that they never arise again.

(ii) An "overcoming", which puts down the cankers and thereby restores mental harmony and purity, here and now, and makes way for future uprooting, if and when cankers arise. By overcoming the cankers repeatedly, they become weakened, not fed, and made to atrophy and die of attrition.

Through overcoming by insight and by development leading to spiritual liberation the cankers are destroyed in the sense of being uprooted.

Through the remaining five methods, namely, overcoming by self-control, judicious use, endurance, avoidance and elimination, the cankers are destroyed in the sense of overcoming, thus making way for uprooting ultimately. In technical terms, while the first two methods accomplish overcoming (*pahāna*) by way of uprooting (*samuccheda*), tranquillisation (*paṭipassaddhi*) and turning away *(nissaraṇa)*, the remaining five methods accomplish it by way of (replacement, *tadaṅga* by a positive alternative) and (calming down) *vikkhambhana.*

The Buddha's teachings of universal flux or changefulness, ultimately boil down to the psychological reality of momentariness. Consciousness is a psychological unit, and it is basically momentary, consisting of three distinct stages–arising (*uppāda*), continuity (*ṭhiti*), passing away (*bhaṅga*). In the backdrop of momentariness, an act of overcoming (*pahāna*) in whatever form amounts to destruction, that is, the non-reappearance of the same phenomenon. There is no such thing as identity; nothing is the same, though there is similarity. Whatever passes away or breaks down cannot reappear, though a similar condition may appear, not once, but indefinitely *until the cause is uprooted.*

The aforesaid seven methods thus constitute a total approach to an all-pervading problem.

The two operative terms on which not only this seven-fold method but the entire theme of the *Sabbāsava Sutta* depends, are *yoniso* and *ayoniso manasikāra*—wise and unwise consideration.

Only when one resorts to wise consideration, that is to say, one views everything according to reality, and not as it appears, can one possibly apply any of these techniques to get rid of a canker. In fact, the cankers arise essentially because attention is focused wrongly and unwisely, conditioning thereby a whole range of warped and unwholesome mental activities, leading to 'the arising of non-arisen cankers, and the stabilization of arisen cankers'. This then is the rationale, wholly objective and result-oriented, of wise consideration. This is how Ācariya Buddhaghosa comments on these two crucial mental operations:

"There, 'wise consideration' means right thinking and attention according to reality. When a thing is impermanent and so on, one considers it as impermanent and so on; this turning of the mind to the actuality of things, the repeated dwelling thereon and the thinking in keeping therewith,—this is called the 'wise consideration'.

"On the other hand 'unwise consideration', is considering in a lop-sided manner, in a basically wrong way. When a thing is impermanent, one considers it to be permanent; when a thing really means affliction, one considers it to be happiness; when a thing is unsubstantial, one considers it to be substantial; when a thing is repulsive, one considers it to be attractive. This kind of wrong consideration or perverted viewing, that is to say, that turning of the mind in contravention of actuality, the repeated dwelling thereon, inclining the mind thereto, the focusing of attention thereon, and thinking to controvert actuality—this is unwise consideration.

"When one understands how wise consideration arises, and one comprehends how unwise consideration does not arise, then does the destruction of cankers occur.

"Now, in order to show the fitness of the rationale, the Buddha has enunciated: 'Monks, for one who unwisely considers, the unarisen cankers arise, and the already arisen cankers increase and monks, for one who wisely considers, the unarisen cankers do not arise and the arisen cankers are overcome.'

"What exactly is meant by this? Cankers arise because one attends to an object in a distorted or wrong way and similarly they are overcome when one attends to an object in a right way. Therefore, one who attends rightly, *i.e.* is able to consider wisely, is one 'who understands' and likewise, one who attends in a way that unwise consideration does not arise is one 'who comprehends'. Briefly, this is what is meant.

"The detailed explanation is as follows: obviously the entire discourse is based on two premises denoted by the terms 'unwise' and 'wise;' in other words, it has been enunciated by way of the round of repeated rebirths, and by way of cessation of the round. The round of phenomenal existence, or repeated birth, death and rebirth, is rooted in unwise consideration and the cessation of the round is rooted in wise consideration. How? Unwise consideration, when indulged in, produces ignorance and craving for becoming; and when ignorance arises, then 'conditioned by ignorance *kamma*-formations arise, conditioned by *kamma*-formations rebirth-consciousness arises' and so on. 'Thus, there comes about the genesis of the whole mass of suffering.' Similarly, when craving occurs, then 'conditioned by craving, clinging arises' etc., and there comes about the genesis of the whole mass of suffering.' (*i.e.,* the law of Dependent Origination).

"Just as a ship is broken, tormented by the fierce smashing of a hurricane, or just as a flock of cattle, while crossing the river, is caught in a whirlpool, or just as oxen tied to the yoke of an oil-mill endlessly circling, even so, a person, given much to unwise consideration, is tied down to and thoroughly enmeshed in the various phenomenal states of existence. He is born, now here, now there, in a certain plane or destiny of a living being, which means that his consciousness is established therein. Thus the round of repeated existence is rooted in unwise consideration.

"Contrarily, when wise consideration is cultivated, one develops the Noble Eightfold Path, spearheaded by Right Understanding, as indicated by the words of the Blessed One 'monks, for a monk who is endowed with wise consideration, this is to be expected, namely, he will develop the Noble Eightfold Path, he will repeatedly practise the Noble Eightfold Path.' Right Understanding here is the penetrating intuitive wisdom or insight. With the flash of this insight, there comes about the extinction of ignorance. 'With the extinction of ignorance, there comes about the extinction of *kamma*-formations etc.; thus there comes about the extinction, without a remainder, of this whole mass of suffering.' (*i.e.*, the Law of Dependent Origination, in the reverse as the mode of cessation). Thus the cessation of the round is to be understood as rooted in wise consideration. Therefore, the entire *Sabbāsava Sutta* is founded on these two premises, denoted by unwise and wise consideration."

It is to be noted here that the above text mentions unwise consideration first, followed by wise consideration. The underlying idea is that the former brings about origination while the latter brings about cessation. As the theme is control, signifying cessation, naturally what originates is mentioned first, and, not *vice versa*.

The commentator makes a very pertinent and insightful observation with reference to how the *āsavas* arise. He says that in this round of aimless wandering, repeated birth, death and rebirth, the starting point of which is inconceivable, there is no such thing as the first beginning of the cankers. All the cankers, in all their myriad ramifications, and in all the varied shades of their pervasiveness, have found berth in a being, somewhere, sometime, repeatedly, in many lives.

So when it is said that an unarisen canker arises, it only means that in the stream of consciousness, characterised by universal flux, a canker arises dependent upon a concatenation of conditions, in a purely empirical sense. By the absence of certain conditions, *i.e.* unwise consideration of a particular nature, a certain canker of a given degree of intensity does not occur.

Conversely, by the presence of those very conditions, the canker arises. So it is all a question of conditionality, the occurrence in a given relation of certain conditions, leading to the presence or absence of cankers.

It is only when the canker is 'burnt out,' so to say, by exposure to intuitive insight, that it ceases once and for all, never to recur, in the same way as a seed, when boiled or burnt, can never sprout again. The seed signifies continuity by its inherent power of reproduction. So has a canker. The analogy of "one whose seed of birth is destroyed" (*khīṇa-bīja*) is just what is meant by the Buddhist concept of the *summum bonum*—Nibbāna—which literally means the "blowing out" of mundane consciousness. This happens when the cankers are totally burnt out (*anāsava*).

Where it is said, "an unarisen canker does not arise", it refers to an ever-present flow of wise consideration, as it has been, for instance, in the case of Thera Mahā Kassapa, as well as Therī Mahā Kapilānī, who were husband and wife in their lay life. It is said that they were reborn as human beings from the exalted state of the radiant Brahma gods. Therefore, from their very childhood, they were exceedingly pure in their thought and conduct. Not even in a dream, not even once, did they experience a thought of sensual desire. That is how, though they were compelled to marry because of the social obligations of the two very well-to-do and aristocratic families, the moment they met, they immediately entered into a pact on living a life of celibacy.

Spiritual purity was a natural bent, a predisposition with them. They just could not be otherwise. Accordingly, on the death of their parents, they distributed all the immense wealth they inherited, became a monk and a nun in the dispensation of the Buddha, and attained to the highest state of sainthood. On gaining the supramundane path and fruition-insights (*lokuttara magga* and *phala*), when their dormant cankers had been totally destroyed, even this possibility of the non-arising of a hitherto 'non-arisen canker,' ceased.

On the other hand, there is the case of a monk, Mahā Tissabhūta Thera by name, a resident of the Maṇḍalārāma monastery. It seems that, motivated by a tremendous spiritual urge, he had entered the Holy Order and was living an exemplary life of spirituality. Once, on his alms-round, he was confronted with the sight of a female that momentarily disturbed the purity of his mind, affecting it by sensual thought. However, he quickly put down the wrong thought. But he was overcome by a sense of remorse that he had become a victim of sensual thought, despite all his sincere and energetic spiritual applications, just because of a momentary lapse in the tempo of mindfulness.

So deeply was he moved at what could have been the painful consequence of a thought if it were allowed to grow, that he forthwith made a vow of uprooting the canker of sensual desire once and for all.

He told himself, "this canker, which had not made its appearance before, has now showed itself: if it is allowed to arise again and again, it will develop and ultimately overpower the mind in such a way that will culminate in my being reborn in the sub-human plane of animals, ghosts etc. This means an endless wandering and a painful involvement in *saṃsāra* (phenomenal existence)."

Thus, seized with a sense of urgency, he plunged himself in meditation as soon as he reached the monastery, and it is said that he soon developed the supramundane insights and became a saint. Thus did he exemplify the Master's teaching: "the arisen canker is destroyed."

What is the criterion whereby one could determine whether a given object or a theme is worthy to be considered or not? Since it is entirely a subjective process, a consideration becomes wise or unwise depending entirely on one's degree of understanding reality. That is to say, one's degree of understanding and comprehending truth in a given set of conditions. Here, it all depends on the individual's discernment, based on his mental perspicuity *vis-a-vis* the three characteristics of impermanence, suffering and non-self or the unsubstantiality underlying all material and mental phenomena.

For a mind properly orientated towards the Dhamma, even a wrong thought or mental object or a wrong conduct, that is, a momentary lapse into something that is unwholesome, can become an incentive for further spiritual edification, as we have seen in the case of Mahā Tissabhūta Thera. Contrarily, a man who does a lot of good, now deliberates wrongly on his good thought or conduct, and thus lapses into a state of self-righteousness and self-deception. Just as in the previous case an unwholesome mental object (*ārammaṇa*), through wise consideration, conduced to wholesome states, so also in the latter case, an *akusala ārammaṇa*, instead of leading one to further *kusala*, only conduced to unwholesome states, because of unwise consideration. What matters, then, is how one considers a given object or theme.

Therefore the commentator rightly says: "whether these things are worthy of consideration or not, there is no definite criterion in terms of their intrinsic quality, though there is in terms of how they are considered."

With reference to the three types of cankers the commentary says: "Here the canker of sense-desire means lust or sensuality based on fivefold objects of sense pleasures. The canker of becoming means that form of desire which hankers after rebirth in the divine realms of the Brahmas (high divinities) with subtle form and beings who are formless. It also means those self-deceptive mystic deviations or wishes (*nikanti*) associated with the attainment of the *jhānas* (meditative absorptions), in that one induces *jhāna* only to enjoy it, as well as those perverted ideological views and dogmas known as the eternalistic belief and annihilistic belief. Thus a fourth canker, that of wrong view, is included here under the canker of becoming. The canker of ignorance means nescience or incomprehension, with reference to the Four Noble Truths.

"There, when one considers in a way that one enjoys the pleasures of the senses, then the unarisen canker of sensual desire arises, and the arisen canker grows. When one considers in a way that one enjoys the sublime or divine states, then the unarisen canker of becoming arises and the arisen canker grows. When one considers all the things pertaining to the three realms of existence on the basis of the fourfold mental distortions (*vipallāsa*) the impermanent to be permanent etc., then the unarisen canker of ignorance arises, and the arisen canker grows. Thus should the arising of the cankers be understood. Likewise, the converse also is true, that the threefold *āsavas* do not arise by wise consideration."

Basically, a canker is a dormant unwholesome tendency or inclination which is an inborn disposition. These tendencies in the mind, continuing since time immemorial, constitute the ingredients of this canker.

A psychological 'seed', with the presence of congenial conditions, sprouts in the form of thoughts, and become stabilized as certain views and adherences. These adherences, in time, get crystallized into dogmas or mental fixations. This mental process, from that of a dormant tendency, *anusaya*, to that of an unshakeable dogma, *diṭṭhi*, is expressed by a very meaningful Pāli term, *abhinivesa*: adherence.

Since *abhinivesa* lays the track of this endless becoming, it is called the 'very stuff' of *saṃsāra*, the vicious circle (*vaṭṭa*) of mundane existence, of birth, death and rebirth. If the mundane is characterized by *kammic* activities rooted in *abhinivesa* or in *anusaya*, the transcendent (*vivaṭṭa*), the dimension of the freedom of Nibbāna, is characterized by the very absence of *abhinivesa* and *anusaya*.

The supramundane insights, with Nibbāna as the object, are thus states of consciousness that systematically uproot and demolish the *abhinivesa* and *anusaya*. *Saṃsāra* can be compared to a stagnant pool, with rotting mire at the bottom which, due to chemical action, constantly sends forth gaseous bubbles to the surface. The mind at the mundane level, with the *āsava* as *abhinivesa*, is very much like such a stagnant rotting pool.

A river with crystal clear water and a swift current never allows any deposit. Its bed is constantly swept clean. The supramundane stream of consciousness performs an analogous function. *Abhinivesas* cannot find a foothold in the dynamic, penetrating insight-stream of the supramundane. And it is for the same reason that no concept, theory or dogma can have any relevance at the supramundane level.

Therefore to cultivate the supramundane, one has to cultivate a rigorous discipline of clear comprehension based on the intuitive penetrative approach, otherwise called "insight meditation," *vipassanā*. The Four Noble Truths constitute the field of *vipassanā*, not as an intellectual base, but as an intuitive experience.

It must be emphasised that the Four Noble Truths, which the Buddha discovered and made known out of compassion, constitute essentially a meditative experience. They are never considered a theory, much less a dogma or scriptural commandment. It is here that Buddhism radically departs from the usual religious stand, in that it bases its main premise on personal experience of the Four Noble Truths, as distinct from divine grace or salvation attained through the intervention of others, whether a God, Teacher, Messiah, Prophet etc.

The first of the seven methods, namely, overcoming through insight, consists of the following:

"This is suffering,' so he wisely considers; 'this is the cause of suffering,' so he wisely considers; 'this is the cessation of suffering,' so he wisely considers; 'this is the path leading to the cessation of suffering,' so he wisely considers. While thus wisely considering, his three fetters are overcome, viz., self-illusion, doubt and clinging to rules and rituals.

"These, monks, are called the cankers to be overcome through (supramundane) insight."

To be successful in developing the supramundane insight, the mind requires to be appropriately oriented. For there is no such thing as 'sudden enlightenment' or sudden access unto the supramundane. The orientation refers to certain basics connected with *vipassanā* meditation. These are:

1. *Sīla-visuddhi*—Purification of morality. This means value orientation, therewith disciplining one's mind and conduct, leading to purification of one's actions, *kamma*, in deed (*kāyena*), word (*vācāya*) and thought (*manasā*). It is *kamma* that involves one in the vicious circle of phenomenal exist-

ence, *saṃsāra*. Therefore it is the cleansing of *kamma*, that forms the first step towards the achievement of spiritual excellence.

2. *Citta-visuddhi*—Purification of mind. This means development of the *jhānas* (absorptions), which is possible only by overcoming the five mental barriers or hindrances (*nīvaraṇa*). These mental barriers are like the high walls which keep one incarcerated within the *kāmaloka*, the world of sense-desires. As soon as these barriers are overcome, one enters into an entirely new and sublime realm, the various stages of ecstatic absorption (*jhāna*) of the divine realm of subtle form (*rūpa-brahma-loka*). This is a multidimensional realm of the high Brahma gods whose consciousness corresponds to the various stages of *jhāna*, attainable through *citta-visuddhi*. One who develops the *jhānic* states, and retains this supernormal attainment, is reborn in the realm of the *rūpāvacara* Brahma gods.

Before one reaches the *rūpāvacara* (sphere of subtle form) states of *jhānas* or *samādhis*, one has to pass through several stages of mental purification. This entire process is called *citta-visuddhi,* the purification of mind. It starts as one begins to meditate. The object on which one initially applies one's mind in meditation is known as *parikamma-nimitta*, initial mental image. The mental onepointedness and composure resulting from this application on the initial object is known as *parikamma-samādhi*—initial concentration.

With increased internalization and mental integration, as unwholesome thoughts and distracting mental images are removed, the mind becomes more and more purified and settled. At this stage, the initial image automatically changes into a pure mentalized image, *uggaha-nimitta*.

For instance, if one is practising the meditation known as *ānāpānasati*, mindfulness of breathing, the initial object is the breath as a tactile sensation. It is a purely sensory object. When this initial object changes into a mentalized one, it is no longer a sensation but the awareness of the sensation which means of a mental object, one step removed from the original.

With the attainment of the mentalized object, the concentration also grows in strength and intensity. This brings greater calmness and inward stillness leading to a further change of the object, and therewith in the level of consciousness. This final change is known as *paṭibhāga-nimitta*, reflex image, which appears in various forms, such as, orb of the sun, bright full moon, twinkling stars, cluster of gems, or just light etc.

The *paṭibhāga-nimitta* is the reflection of the pure state of consciousness. This object cannot be intellectually created. It arises on its own when the mind reaches the required degree of integration and purification. With the arising of the reflex image, the mind enters into the threshold region of the *rūpāvacara*, having overcome the five barriers that hinder its progress upwards.

The *paṭibhāga-nimitta,* thus ushers in the second stage of *samādhi*, known as *upacāra-samādhi*—threshold concentration. From this stage onwards, the five factors of *jhāna* are cultivated, leading to *appanā-samādhi,* ecstatic meditative absorption. There are five stages of *appanā-samādhi*, corresponding to the five *rūpāvacara* states of consciousness.

There are two distinct systems of meditation in Buddhism. One leads to the ecstatic absorptions and supernormal powers arising therefrom. The other leads to the attainment of the supramundane insights, with or without supernormal powers. The former is known as *samatha*—tranquillity meditation–and the latter as *vipassanā,* insight meditation.

*Samatha* literally means 'calmness.' With the attainment of the *jhānas*, the mind acquires profound tranquillity in which the cankers subside or go underground, that is, become dormant. It is like a disturbed and turbid pool becoming calm and clear. All the impurities subside and settle down in the form of sediment. Though the water becomes clear and cool, yet when the pool is whipped up by a storm or disturbed otherwise, the water turns turbid again.

In the same way, though the mind becomes tranquil and

pure by means of *samatha* meditation, yet, since the cankers have not been uprooted by supramundane insights, it can become disturbed and revert into unwholesome states. It is only by cultivating the supramundane insights through *vipassanā* meditation that the cankers are uprooted once and for all, and the consciousness transformed. It is like removing the sediments so as to preclude the possibility of the pool turning turbid again.

To recapitulate, *sīla-visuddhi*, the first of the basics, purifies the mind at the ethical level. And *citta-visuddhi* purifies the mind in its entirety, short of transforming it. Transformation occurs only at the supramundane level through the purification of insight (*ñāṇa-visuddhi*).

The third of the basics starts with the purification of understanding (*diṭṭhi-visuddhi*). This implies right understanding born of the direct experience of the Four Noble Truths; in twelve modes as enunciated by the Buddha in his first discourse, known as Setting in Motion the Wheel of Truth *-Dhammacakka -ppavattana Sutta.*

To purify understanding through *vipassanā*, one has to determine things from the standpoint of ultimate truth, as they really are, and not as they appear to be. That is to say, one views life and everything connected therewith, not in the conventional way, but in its fundamentals.

*Vipassanā* means direct knowledge i.e. knowing in the sense of experiencing. This is different from indirect knowledge *i.e.,* knowing with the aid of concepts, words, symbols, language etc., without actually experiencing the object which one purports to know. While the former is intuitive, the latter is intellectual.

Intellectual or indirect knowledge essentially is information and data, while intuitive or direct knowledge means formation of character and wisdom. With the arising of intuitive insight (*vipassanā*), one directly knows the object, and not about the object; there is a 'flash' which illuminates the consciousness, and one actually experiences and penetrates into the object.

Thus, when life is viewed as an object through *vipassanā*, it is seen (experienced) as *nāmarūpa*–mind and body, not as man, woman, Indian, Chinese, white man, black man etc.

This psychophysical combination is again experienced or seen in terms of certain aggregations known as *khandhas*. These are: *rūpa-khandha*, the aggregate of corporeality; *vedanā-khandha,* the aggregate of feelings; *saññā-khandha*, the aggregate of perceptions; *saṅkhāra-khandha*, the aggregate of mental formations; *viññaṇa-khandha*, the aggregate of consciousness.

The term aggregate has been very meaningfully employed to describe exactly what life is, as an immensely complex and intricate mechanism. This complexity is not intellectually conceived, but seen in actuality intuitively. Further, these five *khandhas* are seen as phenomena constantly arising and passing away, as basically unstable. This dynamic situation, where everything is changing moment to moment (*anicca*), produces the illusion of something that is constant. Continuity itself is mistaken to be constant.

Through the purification of understanding, this illusion is cleared in the same way that mist disappears with the rising of the sun. Insight into the essential instability also opens up the actuality of involvement, and involvement means affliction (*dukkha*), one way or the other. Insight into momentariness and affliction unfolds the truth of unsubstantiality, (*anatta*), that there is no permanent entity underlying all that is changing, all that involves and afflicts. Thus, the basic characteristics (*lakkhaṇas*) or the fundamental features of life, being changeful, affliction-prone and unsubstantial, are intuited as an experience, which profoundly shakes one's very being.

And every time one has this *vipassanā* intuition of life, in terms of the *pañca-khandhas* and the three *lakkhaṇas*, there is a flash within and therewith an electrifying experience. The meditator, with such *vipassanā* experiences, undergoes a change which makes him a different person altogether. No longer can he harbour the familiar illusions, and he hugs no more to false values.

He sees life in terms of the Four Noble Truths, *i.e.,* as the *pañca-khandhas*, subject to the three characteristics which reflect the truth of suffering, the cause of which is a built-in mechanism of the mind itself in the form of the *āsavas*. The dimension of freedom, Nibbāna, is where both suffering and its cause craving, cease and this freedom is reflected during *vipassanā* when the mind is free, at least temporarily, from the *āsavas* and the illusions. Nibbāna is the third truth, the fourth being the Noble Eightfold Path leading unto it which, is meditation (*bhāvanā*) itself supported by morality (*sīla*). Thus, all the Four Truths constitute an integral meditative experience, and not a theory or an intellectual formulation.

The commentary describes the *vipassanā* experience thus: "since all dormant tendencies (*āsavas*) occur only in this process of becoming and not in cessation thereof, one should determine to make this personality, that is, the aggregates, canker-free, beginning with the aggregate of corporeality in this manner: 'in this so-called body there are only the elements of earth, water and the rest.' Having determined one's own personality in terms of the four primary elements, and the derived corporeality arising therewith, one should examine the consciousness and the mental factors which arise making this body their object, and thus comprehend also the four immaterial aggregates (feelings, perceptions, mental formations and consciousness). Thereafter, all these five aggregates are intuitively penetrated in terms of the truth of suffering.

"These five aggregates automatically get reduced to the two principle phenomena of mind and body and the understanding arises that this psycho-physical combination, *nāma-rupa*, is causally originated, comes into being dependent on conditions, by actually identifying the factors, such as ignorance, craving for becoming, mental volition (*manosañce-tanā*), acting as the psychic nutriment etc., thus: 'this is the cause, this the condition, dependent on which the *nāma-rupa* originates.' That is, he penetrates into the underlying characteristics and the functions of both the causative factors and the phenomena arising conditionally therefrom.

"Then he intuitively understands the characteristic of transitoriness by seeing through the changefulness of the phenomena under scrutiny. Then (based upon this experience) he determines the characteristic of suffering by intuiting affliction intrinsic in the oppressive condition of ceaseless rise and fall. Following this experience, he then determines the characteristic of unsubstantiality by intuitively understanding the substancelessness intrinsic in a condition over which one has no hold or control (something that happens on its own, based upon certain conditions, which do not admit intervention of any self or soul). Thus, having grasped the three characteristics, he brings about the arising of the various stages of intuitive insights, one after the other, and thus attains to the supramundane path-insight of Stream-Entrance.

"At the moment of gaining the supramundane path-insight, all the Four Noble Truths are penetrated at once, as an integral experience. This is a victory that is achieved at one stroke of conquest. In that unique moment one penetrates into the truth of suffering by fully and directly comprehending it, penetrates into the cause (of suffering) by uprooting it, penetrates into the cessation (of suffering) by realising it, and penetrates into the path (leading to the cessation of suffering) by developing it.

"In other words, he conquers suffering by means of the conquest of direct and total knowledge, conquers the cause of suffering by means of the conquest of uprooting craving, conquers the realisation of Nibbāna by means of the conquest of cessation of suffering, and conquers the path leading to the cessation of suffering by means of the conquest of development of the Noble Eightfold Path.

"It should be understood that all these victories are not

gained by separate insights, but by just one single insight, which has the truth of cessation, Nibbāna, as the object, and which penetrates the remaining Truths, both as a function and as a conquest. At that moment of victory a thought such as this never occurs to him: 'here I am comprehending suffering, I am uprooting craving, I am realising Nibbāna, I am developing the Noble Eightfold Path, one by one.' But, by making it the object of his insight, as he realises Nibbāna, the very same insight simultaneously comprehends the actuality of suffering, uproots the cause thereof, and develops the path leading to the cessation thereof.

"By means of this insight meditation, as he exercises 'wise reflection,' these three fetters are also instantaneously severed: self-illusion (*sakkāya-diṭṭhi*), comprising the twenty types of wrong views (see SN. XXII 1, 12-16); sceptical doubt (*vicikicchā*), comprising the eight kinds, (as shown in the *Sabbāsava Sutta*); and superstitious belief in rules and rituals (*sīlabbata*), by way of the blind adherence to dogmas and external practices, saying 'purification is brought about only by these rules and these rituals (Sn.1084) and so on.

"Regarding the four cankers: since self-illusion and superstitious belief in rites and rituals are already included in the canker of wrong views, they are both cankers as well as fetters. Sceptical doubt is only a fetter, not a canker. But since it has been included within the method of overcoming through supramundane insight, it is also to be construed as a canker (that is, as a component of the canker of ignorance).

"Now, when the canker of wrong view is overcome, the cankers of sensual desire and of ignorance, which coexist with it in the four unwholesome states of consciousness accompanied by wrong view, are also overcome..."

Thus by *dassanā* (lit. direct vision or experience of Nibbāna), which uproots (*samuccheda*) the first three fetters, the saint attains the first stage of the supramundane path—*Sotāpatti-magga*. Having found access into the transcendental dimension of Nibbāna, through this first supramundane stage, the saint then strives to climb onto the highest spiritual state by attaining to the three remaining stages of supermudane path insights, namely: *Sakadāgāmi-magga*, *Anāgāmi-magga,* and *Arahatta-magga.*

While the first method of overcoming through insight refers to the attainment of *Sotāpatti-magga*, the last method of overcoming through development refers to the attainment of the three remaining path-insights. Even as the first path-insight does away with the three fetters, the remaining three path-insights destroy the remaining seven fetters.

Emancipated from the ten fetters, which tie a being to the various realms of worldly existence, the Arahat becomes the great victor over all cankers, which lay the track into this endless samsāric existence. He is therefore crowned as the Canker-Freed One, who truly is worthy of the highest reverence, offerings and adoration, for he now becomes the "incomparable field of merit for the world," *anuttaraṃ puññakkhettaṃ lokassa.*

Here, the question can be legitimately put: 'If the purpose of freeing the mind of cankers is achieved by the two methods, why then did the omniscient Buddha enunciate five more methods? Do they not become redundant under the circumstances'? The venerable commentator, Ācariya Buddha-ghosa, resolves this question in his inimitable way. The five remaining methods constitute, what he calls, *pubbabhāga-paṭipadā*, the preparatory training or practice. These methods, therefore, are 'applications' that weaken and attenuate the existing fetters and the cankers. They prepare the seeker's mind in a manner as to enable him to undertake his further arduous climb upon the supramundane ranges, crossing peak after peak, each one higher than the previous, until the summit state of spiritual excellence (Arahathood) is reached, opening up the ineffable vista of Nibbāna in all its glory. The four path-insights are the four great peaks of supramundane achievements which provide the utterly perfect and indescribable prospect of Nibbāna. The Path-insights bring about deliverance from *saṃsāra* through the transformation of the consciousness, from the mundane to the supramundane.

An analysis of the five methods constituting the preparatory training have been analysed in the *Visuddhi-magga* by way of these five types of *saṃvara* (control or self-mastery), namely: (1) *Sati-saṃvara* (control through mindfulness); (2) *Ñāṇa-saṃvara* (control through wise consideration); (3) *Khanti-saṃvara* (control through enduring patience); (4) *Sīla-saṃvara* (control through undertaking of precepts); (5) *Viriya-saṃvara* (control through persevering self-effort).

These five types of control are to be understood in the sense of both prevention and fulfilment. By the application of these five methods, each with its specific form of control, (mindfulness, etc.), one secures the mind, protects it from all external dangers and influences. Prevention, therefore, is in the sense of shielding the mind, screening it off from unwholesome factors. A mind thus sheltered from danger becomes easily amenable to a process of cleansing and immunization, brought about by 'fulfilment.'

Thus the various controlling techniques do not amount to "suppressing" oneself, but to restoring unto oneself one's mental health and harmony, and immunizing it from the dangers of the cankers. It is therefore rightly emphasized by the commentator that by these five methods one achieves *vikkhambhana-pahāna,* overcoming through subduing, a prerequisite for the attainment of the supramundane stages.

Each of these five methods is practised only after "wise reflection," which refers to an insightful grasp of the pros and cons of a given situation and a sagacious choice of a technique to deal with it. For instance, when "wisely reflecting, one lives self-controlled by having control over the sense-organ of the eye," and thereby nullifies "cankers which might become destructive and consuming", all one is doing is guarding one's mind, and therewith one's senses. So, "self-control over the senses" does not mean physically controlling or manipulating the various sense-organs. Now, whoever in this world blindfolds himself so that he may have mastery over his faculty of seeing: All he has to do is just be alert mentally; that is, be mindful of what he is seeing, so that he does not allow wrong thoughts to arise based upon what he is seeing. The mindfulness-control, therefore, is basically a psychological technique to be applied sagaciously throughout one's waking hours, in order to keep the mind composed and pure, a prerequisite for the attainment of the supramundane insights.

The application of mindfulness over the senses and the self-mastery resulting therefrom, when viewed from the proper perspective, will reveal a very complex and intricate process of mental development. To begin with, it will unfold, in broad outline, an underlying philosophy determining the choice of these methods because the seeker profoundly understands the consequences by way of unenviable suffering now and later, if these methods are not applied. He or she practises a given technique to meet a challenge.

Therefore, to the seeker no inconveniences, difficulties and sacrifices are too great *vis-a-vis* the grim alternative that would await for failing to practise these methods. The gates of the nether worlds would be wide open with all their unmitigated woes, if the unwholesome states of consciousness are allowed to have their way.

It is this philosophy penetrating into the law of moral causation (*paṭicca-samuppāda*) that ultimately becomes the foundation of all the spiritual endeavour reflected by these methods. If one is advised to make judicious use of the basic needs of life or patiently to endure harsh and unpleasant experiences, even acute physical suffering, or avoid evil association, unseemly places and wild creatures, or eliminate any unwholesome or wrong thought, it is because only by doing so the "cankers which might become destructive and consuming", do not become destructive and consuming owing to these applications.

Clearly, then, there are two very practical objectives which are aimed at by these applications. The five methods of self-control (*saṃvara*) being the five applications, each with the two objectives of prevention of the arising of canker on the one hand and fulfilment through the attainment of canker-free state. Cankers are like fires in the mind. One needs to extinguish this fire. For, if not promptly put out, it would grow into a mighty conflagration and swallow everything that falls on its raging path: that is, become destructive and consuming.

By applying these fivefold methods, one averts a would-be calamity, the magnitude of which cannot be conceived. This is like taking prompt and timely action to put out a fire. By such action as one prevents the cankers from arising, one also fulfils the task of purifying and composing the mind, thus rendering the cankers and the concomitant defilements ineffective. Once the cankers are made ineffective by not being fed, their power is attenuated, so much so that with the cultivation of the *vipassanā* insights, these greatly weakened mental effluents and fetters get destroyed by the arising of the supramundane path-insights.

The venerable commentator also provides instances to show the effectiveness of these methods. They are case-histories of Buddhist *yogis* who, through sheer sincerity of purpose and unreserved commitment, succeeded in practising these methods under very trying circumstances and attained to the summit spiritual state of the Arahat. For instance, there is the case of Venerable Lomasanāga Thera. He practised patient endurance in its most acute form and stuck to his meditation never giving up effort even for a moment. Perspiring profusely in midsummer and undergoing difficulties of all kinds unbendingly he pursued his noble pursuit. To practise endurance he would contemplate by mentally visualizing the innumerable times during his endless wandering in the circle of becoming (*saṃsāra*) he was swallowed by other creatures. Living in the midst of a cruelly competitive world ruled by the law of tooth and claw, how many times he had been beheaded by enemies; how many times he had undergone excruciating pain and suffering life after life. And he would wonder, "Still this recurring existence continues in all its might, and laden by the mystery of unpredictability! How long must I go through this?" Thinking this way, he endured great difficulties in fulfilment of his spiritual pursuit until he became an Arahat.

"There is further the case of Venerable Padhāniya Thera. Though he had suffered the murderous sting of a poisonous snake, he cheerfully continued in his efforts, notwithstanding the sharp and shooting pains, until his endeavours were crowned with success, right at the penultimate moment before he actually passed away as an Arahat.

These great *yogis* preferred death to compromises and to the machinations of a deceptive mind. This only highlights the need for a total dedication to these methods, based upon a clear comprehension of their purpose and possibilities. A lukewarm undertaking only fouls up one's pursuit.

In the portion dealing with the elimination of wrong and unwholesome thoughts, the *Sabbāsava Sutta* mentions three specific wrong thoughts, *i.e.,* thoughts of sensual pleasure, ill-will and cruelty, which a seeker "gets rid of, eliminates, makes an end of and liquidates." The Sutta also mentions "He does not endure any evil and unwholesome mental states, whenever they may arise." The Commentary specifies "any evil and unwholesome mental condition," in terms of six wrong and unwholesome thoughts.

These are:

(I) *Ñāti-vitakka*, a thought concerning one's relatives and dear ones; i.e. a thought rooted in attachment, possessiveness, infatuation, fear, worry, resentment etc.,

(2) *Janapada-vitakka*, a thought concerning one's native land, that is a thought rooted in pride, false views, attachment, sentimentalism etc.,

(3) *Amara-vitakka*, a thought or speculation concerning the deathless, that is, a thought rooted in ideological perversity, bigotry, intolerance etc.,

(4) *Parānudayatā-paṭisamyutta-vitakka*, a thought concerning others' kindness etc. That is, a thought rooted in sentimental and sensual attachment, worldly affection etc.,

(5) *Lābha-sakkāra-siloka-paṭisamyutta-vitakka*, a thought concerning gain, honour and reputation; that is, a thought rooted in acquisitiveness, greed, arrogance, pride etc.,

(6) *Anavaññatti-paṭisamyutta-vitakka*, a thought of not being despised, surpassed; that is, thought rooted in inferiority complex or conceit, arrogance, egotism etc..

A careful analysis of these nine types of thought will throw tremendous light on the working of the human mind. In fact, these are the thoughts which, when allowed a free rein, grow into blind prepossessions and obsessions that invariably lead to various mental ailments. The causes for schizophrenia and paranoia are to be found in these wrong thoughts and mental conditionings.

The seeker, the commentator says, does not allow wrong thoughts because he clearly sees the dangers inherent in such mental activities. He comprehends how one thing leads to another, and how the mind itself is rendered sick and utterly debilitated, unless one consciously and deliberately gets rid of, eliminates and liquidates, makes an end of such thoughts whenever they may arise. Thus the elimination is brought about not through some theory, sentiment or ideology, but through right understanding and unrelenting application. The practical lessons arising from many such observations of the commentator, thus, are indeed priceless. Right thought leads to right aspiration, and both these are based on right understanding. The psychological importance of a method, which enables one through all one's normal routine activities to develop insight, the highest wisdom, therefore, can never be emphasized adequately.

*Āsavas* die hard. Even though rendered inactive by *vikkhambhana-pahāna*, overcoming through meditative elimination of mental hindrances, that is, though stripped of their active and ominous power, they continue to smoulder as dormant tendencies or compulsions (*abhinivesa*) in ever so many mysterious and confusing guises. That is how they create self-deceptions and predispose the consciousness towards extremes, in one way or the other. Until the supramundane path-insight is attained by the transformation of consciousness, enabling one to transcend the possibility of falling back to the mundane, the *āsavas*, even as latent forces, pursue the seeker in diverse ways as so many impeding mental conditions and afflictions (*upaddava*).

In fact, one of the definitions of the term *āsava* is *upaddava*: affliction, distress, calamity, misery etc. That the *āsavas* in their active, potent form, *i.e.*, as unwholesome *kammas*, wreak on oneself all the havoc, misfortunes and sufferings, is clear enough. However, what the *āsavas,* as dormant forces, are capable of inflicting is not evident.

It is like the case of a toothless and clawless tiger turned man-eater. Though the beast has been deprived of its weapons, by sheer brute-force it can still overwhelm and frighten away even formidable foes. By causing the mind to fluctuate between extremes of all kinds—now becoming slothful, now restless; now rigid, now loose; now prone to self-indulgence and now to self-mortification, now given to eternalism, now to nihilism—these dormant, unwholesome tendencies afflict the seeker right up to the very bounds that separate the supramundane from the mundane.

It is only by wielding the almighty armour of the seven Enlightenment Factors of Mindfulness, Investigation of Dhamma, Effort, Rapture, Tranquillity, Meditative Concentration and Equanimity that the seeker is able to get rid of these afflictions. The Enlightenment Factors, being diametrically opposed to the unwholesome cankers and defilements, represent the wholesome equivalents or antipodal good forces

(*Dhamma-sāmaggi*), and it is by virtue of this capacity that they can withstand, resist, and effectively counteract the afflictions in all forms.

Why are these seven factors so specifically given this meaningful and reverential appellation of Enlightenment Factors? Because these seven factors, when fully developed and orchestrated, climax into that supreme, self-transforming spiritual experience called Enlightenment.

The implications are that they are factors both contributory to, as well as concomitants of, Enlightenment. Therefore, it is said, *sati, dhammavicaya, viriya, pīti, passaddhi, samādhi, upekkhāsaṅkhātāya dhammasāmaggiyā-ariyasāvako bujjhatī'ti bodhi*—"it is Enlightenment in that the noble disciple awakens unto 'truth' by the orchestration of the enlightenment factors of mindfulness, investigation of Dhamma, effort, rapture, tranquillity, meditative concentration and equanimity."

The Commentator defines the term "awakens" thus:

(a) *kilesa-santāna-niddāya uṭṭhahatī'ti*—"Awakens means one wakes up from the slumber of the defilements."

(b) *cattāri vā ariyasaccāni paṭivijjhatī'ti* — "One penetrates into or fully comprehends, the Four Noble Truths."

(c) *nibbānameva vā sacchikarotī'ti*—"One realizes (directly experiences) Nibbāna, the Summum Bonum."

Thus, awakening or becoming enlightened, which reflects the crescendo, so to say, of the orchestration of the seven *Bojjhaṅgas*, signifies a very unambiguous and clear cut summit of spiritual experience. It means that at the moment when Enlightenment takes place, as one dispels the slumber of defilements, that is, uproots the cankers, one also simultaneously penetrates into, *i.e.*, discovers, the Truths concerning both the state of bondage and its cause, and the dimension of liberation and the means thereunto; and this happens with the direct experience of Nibbāna.

The unique role of the Enlightenment Factors, both as

instruments leading to Nibbāna and as components of the supramundane insights, is clear also from this succinct definition: *bodhiyā bodhissa vā aṅgo'ti bojjhaṅgo*, "because it leads or contributes to Enlightenment, or because it is the component of Enlightenment, it is called an Enlightenment Factor."

The most significant concept underlying these definitions is that of *dhammasāmaggi*—the orchestration, concordance, unity or harmony of seven distinctly independent spiritual elements. Like the combination of simultaneous notes, these spiritual elements form, so to say, that chord or harmony called Enlightenment. Though a single experience, Enlightenment is the confluence of spiritual insights forming the fourfold facets of the Noble Truths. In other words, it is the climactic moment that converges onto Nibbāna, that is to say, realizes Nibbāna as the transcendent object of the supramundane consciousness.

The uniqueness of the teachings of the Buddha lies also in this concept of orchestration, signifying a spiritual discovery, a self-realization, to be attained by each seeker through unreserved commitment and self-effort. In theistic religions, the emphasis is on the grace or intervention of a supernatural agency or God, which renders self-effort and individual spiritual discovery superfluous. On the contrary, this concept of orchestration underlines the need for individual excellence coupled with self-discovery, thereby making extraneous influence irrelevant.

Whereas the intervention of an external agency is always rooted in fear and blind faith, leading to bigotry and religious wars, the Buddha's teachings of orchestration of an individual's spiritual endowments are always rooted in hope, self-confidence and rational approach and have never led to bigotry or sectarian violence. The practical and the social importance of this concept of orchestration, therefore, can never be highlighted enough.

The next question is, "Why must these spiritual endowments be only seven, not less, not more"? This is directly related to what may be called the dichotomous nature of life and the world, and therewith the dichotomous working of the mind, conditioned as it is by the world around. Mind, by its very nature, tends to swing between pairs of opposites–love-hate, hilarity-depression, immobility-overactivity etc. A little thoughtfulness should be more than enough, even for the most unsophisticated and unlettered mind, to discern the bipolar nature of one's mental inclinations.

Supremely realistic as the Buddha was, he formulated these Enlightenment Factors in keeping with this basic dualism. Wisdom lies in taking the line of least resistance. So, instead of fighting against a tendency that is well-entrenched in one's mind, it is always better to make use of the same force in a way as to further one's spiritual growth. Having this in mind, the Buddha enunciated not only these seven factors but also arranged them in a manner that corresponds precisely to the realities and needs of spiritual development.

It is to be clearly understood that the mind swings contrariwise exactly in response to the mutually opposing psychological forces of what may be called contraction and distraction, or immobility (*līna*) and over-activity (*uddhacca*). While the former induces a constricted, shrunken and dull condition, the latter produces a dilated, restless and excited state. Whether it is the unresponsive or sluggish condition or the over-enthusiastic or agitated one, both signify an unbalanced and muddled state and it is only the Enlightenment Factors which can lift the mind from this distorted, uncreative and dichotomous situation.

Says the Commentator:

*Kasmā pana Bhagavatā satteva bojjhaṅgā vuttā anūnā anadhikāti. Līnuddhacca-paṭipakkhato sabbatthikato ca. Ettha hi tayo bojjhaṅgā līnassa paṭipakkhā. Tayo uddhaccassa paṭipakkhā. Eko panettha sabbatthiko.*

"But why have only seven Enlightenment Factors been enunciated by the Blessed One, not less and not more? By way of their being antithetical to the extremes of dullness and disquiet, as also by way of being the common factor beneficial to all. Now, while three factors of Enlightenment are diametrically opposed to the dull or inactive inclination, three others counteract the disquiet or over-active tendency of the mind, and one functions as the common factor beneficial to all."

The tendency towards dullness or the inactivity or immobility of mind is characterised by these three features:

(1) Mental blindness, stupidity, ignorance, delusion.
(2) Sluggishness, laxity, indolence.
(3) Dejection, depression, sadness, melancholia.

Mental blindness naturally produces doubt, cynicism, scepticism, confusion and inner incertitude. The only antidote for this is discernment and comprehension arising from objective evaluation and investigation of the phenomena causing doubt. In *Dhamma-vicaya* the term *Dhamma* (phenomena), to be precise, refers to *nāmarūpa*, the psycho-physical complex called personality and this factor is the one sure panacea for the removal of mental blindness. Sluggishness and indolence can be overcome only by effort. Dejection and depression are easily destroyed by cultivating rapture.

The tendency towards the disquiet or the over-activity of mind is characterised by these three features:

(1) Agitation, excitement, restlessness.
(2) Distraction, or a fragmented, scattered state (of mind).
(3) Disequilibrium, instability, changefulness.

Agitation is removed by the cultivation of tranquillity, distraction by meditative concentration and instability by equanimity.

Dullness and disquiet respectively signify under-balanced and over-balanced conditions, hence lack of equilibrium. They are both unbalanced states of consciousness, which must necessarily produce disharmony and bewilderment. The six factors which counteract these two extremes with their specific features, as mentioned above, are able to do so because of the support of mindfulness which acts as an equaliser. This fact is made abundantly clear by the Enlightened One himself in the following discourse found in the Saṃyutta Nikāya. (S.V, 114).

*Yasmiṃ ca kho bhikkhave, samaye līnaṃ cittaṃ hoti, kālo tasmiṃ samaye dhammavicaya-sambojjhaṅgassa bhāvanāya, kālo viriya-sambojjhaṅgassa bhāvanāya kālo pīti-sambojjhaṅgassa bhāvanāya.*

*Yasmiṃ ca kho bhikkhave, samaye uddhataṃ cittaṃ hoti, kālo tasmiṃ samaye passaddhi-sambojjhaṅgassa bhāvanāya, kālo samādhi-sambojjhaṅgassa bhāvanāya, kālo upekkhā-sambojjhaṅgassa bhāvanāya.*

*Satiñca kvāhaṃ, bhikkhave, sabbatthikaṃ vadāmīti*

"Monks, when the mind is in a state of dullness, then that is the time for the development of the Enlightenment Factor of Investigation of Dhamma, time for the development of the Enlightenment Factor of Effort, time for the development of the Enlightenment Factor of Rapture.

"Monks, when the mind is in a state of disquiet, that is the time for the development of the Enlightenment Factor of Tranquillity, time for the development of the Enlightenment Factor of Meditative Concentration, time for the development of the Enlightenment Factor of Equanimity.

"Monks, Mindfulness is what I call the common factor beneficial to all."

This is how the Enlightenment Factors in the context of universal dichotomy occasion equilibrium and harmony, and then are orchestrated to climax into Enlightenment. Mindfulness has been very significantly placed as the first of these Enlightenment Factors, since it is the equalizer between pairs of opposites—between the credulous and the cynical, the indolent and the over-active, the introvert and the extrovert etc.

*Sati* acts as the ballast of the ship of mind upon the sea of *saṃsāric* existence. Arising out of this is the unique Buddhist concept of *indriya samatha*—equalization of the spiritual faculties. A person given overmuch to devotional practices tends towards blind faith. Similarly, a person given overmuch to purely intellectual pursuit of religion tends towards cynicism and hypocrisy. But, when a person integrates devotion with wise consideration, based upon investigation of Dhamma, he or she brings about an equalization of the spiritual faculties and thereby a harmonious development.

Likewise if a seeker, due to an excess of zeal, exerts too much, he or she will only succeed in becoming over-anxious, excited and irritable, thereby mismanaging the spiritual life thoroughly. On the contrary, if he or she is too easy-going and expects spiritual excellence through external aids, he or she will surely end up in frustration and superstition.

Here equalization of spiritual faculties would mean a fusion of the devotional approach with right understanding, of exertion with equipoise, of self-confidence with self-effort. This can be done only when one is fully committed to the development of mindfulness. Mindfulness and clear comprehension, it is to be reminded, are twins. One is always accompanied and supported by the other, leading to what the commentator calls "Awakenment."

When one awakens to the Truth, one becomes wide awake to the realities represented by this Truth. Enlightenment is never a sudden affair, though it may appear to be so. It is always the culmination of a process of development and self-culture. Thus, when one is wide awake, the consciousness, like an ever-widening spiral, keeps on waking to a vision of Nibbāna, and this waking becomes clearer with each higher step in the attainment of path-insights, and when consciousness, by this progressive unfoldment of the supramudane prospect of Nibbāna reaches full awakenment, it reaches the peak of Arahathood.

The *Paṭisambhidā-magga*, as quoted by the commentator,

describes this process of progressive awakenment in the following manner:

1. *Bujjhatī'ti bodhi*—"One awakens unto truth,therefore it is Enlightenment." This may be construed as representing *sotāpatti-magga*—the supramundane path-insight of Stream-entry.

2. *Anubujjhatī'ti bodhi* —"One is wide awake unto Truth, therefore it is Enlightenment.," This may be construed as representing *sotāpatti-phala*—the supramundane fruition-insight of Stream-entry.

3. *Paṭibujjhatī'ti bodhi* — "One, keeps on waking unto Truth, therefore it is Enlightenment." This may be construed as representing five more *lokuttara* supramundane-stages of path and fruition-insights (*sakadāgāmi-magga* and *-phala*, *anāgāmī-magga* and *-phala*, and *arahatta-magga*).

4. *Saṃbujjhatī'ti bodhi*—"One is fully awakened unto Truth, therefore it is Enlightenment." This may be construed as representing the summit state of fruition-insight of Arahathood (*arahatta-phala*).

Thus, like an ever-widening spiral, at four distinct levels, from *Sotāpatti* to *Arahatta*, through the dual viewpoints, so to say, of path and fruition-insights, *magga-phala-ñāṇa,* the process of awakenment is orchestrated by the seven Enlightenment Factors.

It is interesting to note that each of these seven Factors of Enlightenment "is based" upon detachment, dispassion, and cessation, and matures into abandonment." The Pāli words for detachment etc., are *viveka*, *virāga*, *nirodha* and *vossagga* respectively. Tremendously meaningful, each term again signifies a specific mode of mental freedom and spiritual liberation.

It has been mentioned that there are various modes of overcoming (*pahāna*), representing a process of release of the mind from the bondage created by the fetters, which are overcome. These are overcoming by way of substituting the evil with good etc.

The commentator also divides detachment, dispassion and cessation into five distinct modes, which are identical with those explained under overcoming. These are as follows:

1. *Tadaṅga-viveka*—

By substituting evil with good, one conduces detachment.

2. *Vikkhambhana-viveka*—

By subduing the five mental hindrances (*nīvarana*) one composes the mind and therewith conduces detachment.

3. *Samuccheda-viveka*—

By uprooting the fetters (*saṃyojana*), through *magga-ñāṇa* one conduces detachment.

4. *Paṭippassaddhi-viveka*—

By tranquillization of the mind through *phala-samāpatti*, one conduces detachment.

5. *Nissaraṇa-viveka*—

By "escaping" from the hold of the cankers, and thus of worldly existence, through the realization of Nibbāna, one conduces detachment.

The first two modes of detachment are mundane, *lokiya*, while the remaining three are supramundane, *lokuttara*. As in the case of *viveka* (detachment), *virāga* (dispassion) and *nirodha* (cessation) too are identically fivefold.

In terms of the seven methods, the first and last, being *lokuttara*, correspond to the last three modes, (*samuccheda* etc.) while the five intermediate methods, as preparatory or *lokiya* steps, correspond to the first two modes (*tadaṅga-vikkhambhana*).

The *Bojjhaṅgas* are said to "mature into abandonment." Here abandonment is two-fold:

(1) By way of giving up (*pariccāga*) defilements and therewith worldly bondage.

(2) By way of advancement upon the supramundane way, as one leaps forward (*pakkhandana*) towards Nibbāna.

In other words, as the commentator says, *Yatthā kilese pariccajati-nibbānañca pakkhandati* —"As one gives up, abandons, one also advances towards Nibbāna," both processes being correlative.

The seven methods of the *Sabbāsava Sutta* succeed quite well in revealing this progressive unfoldment through the development and orchestration of individual spiritual endowments and excellences, by presenting them in the order it does. The first method of overcoming through supramundane insight represents *sotāpatti-magga*. The last method of overcoming through development of the *Bojjhaṅgas* represents the seven remaining *lokuttara-ñāṇas* (supramundane insights). The five methods in-between represent a preparatory course of cleansing and strengthening of consciousness.

Now, what exactly is meant by the term "development" of the *Bojjhaṅgas*? That is, how are the *Bojjhaṅgas* developed? A *Bojjhaṅga* basically is a mental factor (*cetasika*). Out of the seven *Bojjhaṅgas*, three i.e., *viriya*, *pīti* and *samādhi* (*ekaggatā*), are common to all states of consciousness (*aññasamāna*). The remaining four, i.e., *sati*, *dhammavicaya* (*paññā*), *passaddhi*, *upekkhā* (*tatra-majjhattatā*), pertain only to wholesome (*kusala*) states of consciousness. Development of these mental factors, which co-exist with consciousness, should be understood only in the sense of repetitive action or arising. That is to say, these factors should be repeatedly aroused by appropriate spiritual practice. Says the commentator:

*Bhāvetī'ti vaḍḍheti, attano cittasantāne punappunaṃ janeti abhinibbattetī'ti attho* - "One develops' means one cultivates them. That is, one rouses them, brings them to being repeatedly in one's stream of consciousness."

# Chapter 4

## The Canker-free
## Khīṇasāva

The goal of life according to the *Dhammapada*.

### I

Life, according to the Dhammapada, has meaning only when there is a purpose for living. This goal should be truly beyond the reach of the forces that, within a vicelike grip, hold one in phenomenal existence. The philosophy projected by the *Dhammapada*, in broad outlines, can be put thus:

Be like birds in the air!
Untraceable, leaving no marks,
Upon the shifting sands of time,
That birth, death and rebirth conjure,
Upon this universal flux of *saṃsāra*,
Try not to leave the footmark of 'I'.

This makeshift nest called life,
Substantial though it may seem,
Is a bubble, kamma-wrought,
Liberated be from this empty toilsomeness.

Ever oozing is the canker:
Breeding a circle, endless and aimless,
So like the bird, free be!

The Dhammapada is the spiritual testament of the Buddha. Flashes of insight that illuminated the Buddha-heart have been crystallized into luminous verses of pure wisdom. As the Buddhist manual of right living, the Dhammapada is a world classic and a perennial source of inspiration.

The basic concepts of Buddhism have been marshalled in this resume of the sacred Pāli Canon, in a way that even a simple, unsophisticated seeker of truth can benefit from, as much as, or perhaps more than, a scholar burdened with the weight of learning. Thus, in the Dhammapada the *āsavas* have been depicted by images that are full of wisdom.

In a desert no man in his senses would make a given sand dune a fixed reference point to guide caravans. Sand dunes shift often and where there is a hill today, there could be a big depression tomorrow. Life, wrought by *kamma* and fraught with suffering, is at best a tracing, a temporary track laid by the *āsavas*, only to be obliterated.

If *āsava* is the ink, life is the imprint or impression thereof, rather a heavy one, which, 'bleeding through', leaves its mark on the next page. The page called "life", lightly printed, with further *āsava* imprints or activities, similarly impresses the subsequent pages.

The idea of oozing, seeping or percolating is bound up with the idea of layers, levels, areas and time. This is exactly what the concept of life is in Buddhism, that is, a process or progression from life to life, through different planes of existence, through different levels and modes of psycho-physical formation. This dynamic imagery of life is called *saṃsāra*, wandering, in the sense of aimless drifting or existential vagrancy.

In the Dhammapada, *āsava* is a synonym of *saṃsāra*, endless wandering. It emphasizes an existential situation which has neither permanent footing nor purpose. *Āsava*, effluent or discharge, by its very nature, percolates without a purpose, pollutes without provocation, plagues without punishing, perplexes without persecuting. Even so it is with *saṃsāra*. By its very changeful, impersonal and conditioned nature, it perpetuates a perennial stream of discrete, discontinuous, distinct, individual units of becoming called 'life.'

*Saṃsāra*, like a wound, is an affliction needing to be tended. Until healed, a wound, whence matter is continuously discharged, is an affliction, an illness. Āsava is a mental wound, from which mental discharges continuously ooze, and therefore signifing affliction. And affliction requires to be tended. *Āsavas* are also tended by continuous 'feeding.' Feeding, *āhāra*, is a synonym of *āsava* and therefore also of *saṃsāra*.

The word *āhāra*, "feeding", is a technical term in Buddhism, with very pregnant philosophical implications, something which sustains and perpetuates *āsava* as well as *saṃsāra*. There are four *āhāras*, one physical and the other three mental. These *āhāras* sustaining the mind and body (*nāma-rūpa)* can be described as psycho-physical processes of feeding the continuity of phenomenal existence. As such they represent a dynamic universal law, known as *Niyāma Dhamma*, cosmic laws that govern all forms of sentient existence. The working of *āhāras,* in conjunction with *niyāma-dhammas,* are as follows:

1. *Kavalīkāra āhāra*—Physical nourishment as bodily feeding representing the laws of physical nature which regulate seasonal changes, environmental balance (*utu-niyāma),* and reproductive functions *(bīja-niyāma) etc.*

2. *Phassāhāra*—Sensory and mental contact or impression as mental feeding representing *citta-niyāma*, law that governs the working of mind.

3. *Manosañcetanāhāra*—Volitional activity as kammic feeding representing *kamma-niyāma*, the law that governs the relationship between action and its result. *e.g.* rebirth.

4. *Viññāṇāhāra*—Consciousness that links the previous life with the subsequent as existential food representing *Dhamma -niyāma*, the law that governs one's destiny both here and

hereafter, as also the supernormal events, attainments etc.

These four types of *āhāra* amount to a process of feeding the body, the mind, *kamma* and rebirth, and thus sustain and perpetuate *āsava*, and thereby *saṃsāra*.

The *Dhammapada*, by setting a goal, spells it out very concretely. The only meaningful goal of life, and therefore also the true objective for all spiritual endeavour, is what is called *khīṇāsava*, the canker-free state. A wise caravan leader has for guidance the pole star, or some such reliable reference point, as he travels through infinite stretches of perilous and arid desert, made more fearsome by the countless carcasses strewn all over, of those victims who, losing the way, lost their lives. Similarly, the seeker of truth should have the three *vimokkhas*, leading to the *khīṇāsava* state, as the only reliable instrument or guide for his or her journey through the desert of *saṃsāra* unto Nibbāna. *Vimokkhas* are the positive antipodes of the *āsavas*, as mentioned in the *Sabbāsava Sutta*. The three *vimokkhas* have been fully discussed in the chapters: 1. Destruction of Cankers, 2. Canker and Deliverance (pages . . . and. . .).

## The Arahat Anuruddha

There are quite a number of verses in the Dhammapada which directly deal with *āsava*. They clearly show the exalted transmundane state where the *āsavas* come to an end, as well as the practical methods leading to it. These guidelines enable a practitioner to make a resolute, steady, step-by-step advancement from the *āsava*-polluted *saṃsāra* to that dimension utterly cleansed of *āsava*, Nibbāna.

There are at least ten verses that clearly enunciate both the goal and the path. There are also numerous verses dealing with *āsava*, partially and indirectly or along with other themes. The most interesting and instructive aspect of the Dhammapada, however, is the abundant light it throws on the attributes, the specific qualities of those who have become *khiṇāsavas*. What exactly happens to a *khiṇāsava*, how he conducts himself, how he influences and affects society these are questions of tremendous practical importance. And the *Dhammapada* answers them lucidly indeed.

And to that extent, if ever a book can be called a friend, a philosopher and a guide, it is the *Dhammapada*. To the simple and unsophisticated devotee, the *Dhammapada* is like unto a sympathetic and understanding counsellor, to the erudite scholar, bearing the academic burden, its pithy and wise sayings exert a most sobering effect, even as a true philosopher humbles a pretentious intellectual. And to the earnest seeker of truth it is a guide *par excellence*.

The stanza which most forcefully, clearly and eloquently presents the basic philosophy of the *Dhammapada*, *vis-a-vis* the *āsavas*, is the ninety-third *gāthā*. The Blessed One pronounced this verse as the epilogue of a discourse which he gave while staying at Veluvana, the famous royal bamboo grove at Rājagaha, gifted by King Bimbisāra of Magadha. The Buddha declared:

*Yassāsavā parikkhīṇā*
*āhave ca anissito:*
*suññato animitto ca*
*Vimokkho yassa gocaro*
*ākāse'va sakuntānam*
*padaṃ tassa duranhayaṃ*

Dhp.93

He whose cankers are destroyed,
Who is no longer bound by food,
Who only resorts to that spiritual deliverance,
The void and the unconditioned Nibbāna,.
His path is untraceable,
Like that of birds in the air.

This discourse, in fact, had a very interesting background,

concerned with the Venerable Anuruddha, one of the eighty great disciples (*Mahāsāvaka*), who had been under great pressure by envious and censorious monks. Venerable Anuruddha was a first cousin of the Buddha. He was brought up in great luxury, and was actually chosen as the heir-apparent of the Sakya Kingdom, of which Gotama himself would have become the monarch, had he not renounced the throne to become the Buddha, the Monarch of Dhamma (*Dhammarāja*).

Venerable Anuruddha was so greatly inspired by the exalted example of the Tathāgata (Bearer of Truth), that he too decided to renounce the world to discover the Truth himself. For a most delicate prince to take to the ascetic life of a monk caused great misgiving in the minds of his parents, relatives and friends.

Undaunted, Venerable Anuruddha plunged into a life of seclusion marked by austerity and abstemiousness in a remote forest hermitage. He lived on alms-meal collected from the poorest and humblest of folks living in forest hamlets and remote villages. He wore *paṃsukūla* robes made out of pieces of cloth thrown in cremation grounds and in refuse heaps by the people. He stitched the discarded cloths into robes and dyed them in a concoction made out of barks collected from the forest trees. He lived in a hut made of bamboo and thatch. Apart from what he wore, and the begging-bowl, he possessed nothing,

Soon Venerable Anuruddha climbed upon the summit of Arahathood, together with great supernormal attainments, and became pre-eminent among the wielders of the supernormal power called Divine Eye *(dibbacakkhu)*. With all his greatness and spiritual powers he was known for his compassion and love for the suffering beings. True to the teaching of his Master, he wandered from place to place, preaching the Dhamma 'for the welfare of the many, for the happiness of the many.' Though he had a large following of devotees all over the country, he did not stay in any one place too long, not even in his forest hut.

Once it so happened that as his robes had literally become threadbare he went in search of discarded cloth in refuse-heaps. Suddenly in one of the heaps he saw the corner of a cloth sticking out. On pulling he found three rolls of cloth, sufficient for a full set of robes. It was a pleasant surprise for him, and he exclaimed, "What an excellent piece of *paṃsukūla* cloth."

A *paṅsukula* literally means a cloth thrown away in cremation grounds, that is, something discarded as useless. Only those monks who prefered the most austere life undertaking the various ascetic practices, wore the *paṃsukūla* robes.

It is said that this particular roll of *paṃsukūla* was laid by a certain goddess, Jālinī by name, of the Tāvatiṃsa divine realm. Venerable Anuruddha was a monk of great merit and was therefore much revered, not only by human beings but also by the divine beings. And goddess Jālinī happened to be related to him in the past, being his wife in his third previous birth.

The account of this event in the *Dhammapada* Commentary is most interesting. It seems, when Venerable Anuruddha was looking for some *paṃsukūla*, goddess Jālinī, noticing it, quickly materialized the required quantity of cloth and thought to herself, "If I offer this cloth openly to the Elder, he probably will not accept it. Let me therefore hide it in one of those heaps lying ahead of him" aṇd thus by her supernormal powers, she hid the cloth in the refuse-heap so as to be accessible to the Venerable Elder.

The Buddha became aware of how this wonderful offering came to be made and accordingly there was a special occasion for making a set of robes for Venerable Anuruddha. The Buddha himself and his eighty pre-eminent disciples, together with the five hundred chosen monks, went to the monastery where this material was spread out for making a robe. Venerable Sāriputta, Venerable Mahā Moggallāna, Venerable Mahā Kassappa and Venerable Ānanda, took their positions around the cloth and the Master himself inaugurated the proceedings by threading the needle.

As all the monks engaged themselves in cutting and stitching the cloth, goddess Jālinī went to the nearby village to rouse the inhabitants. She projected the thought in them, saying, "Friends, to make the robe for our noble Elder Anuruddha, the Master himself, his eighty pre-eminent disciples, together with five hundred chosen monks, have gathered in your monastery. Please take advantage of this great opportunity of acquiring the rarest of merit by way of offering alms-food to this unique assembly of noble saints, with the Buddha at the head. Go to the monastery and offer alms."

Thus, becoming aware of the presence of the Buddha and the saints, with a tremendous sense of urgency and devout faith, all the inhabitants prepared the purest of meals they possibly could prepare within the available time. Then, carrying the food to the monastery exulting in sheer rapture, they offered this alms meal. After the alms meal, there was a great quantity of left-over food.

As the elders busied themselves to complete the task of robe-making in time, a few monks became critical of what was happening. They made a false accusation, saying, "Why should such huge quantities of food be made to be brought? Would it not have been proper that only after assessing the required quantity that the relatives and devotees were instructed to bring only that much etc."? In order to advertise what a great circle of relatives and devotees he has, the Elder Anuruddha must have had so much food brought."

Though scandalous, the accusation only evoked a response of sympathetic understanding in those great saints. They knew that even the sun and the moon must suffer being enshrouded by dark, though passing, clouds. And a spiritual giant such as the Venerable Anuruddha had to face undeserving criticisms from unenlightened people.

The Buddha, in his boundless compassion, made use of the occasion not only to dispel the evil that had overpowered the minds of those monks, but, even more importantly, to reveal the glory that the canker-free state bestows on those who have achieved the highest excellence.

Accordingly, the Master asked those fault-finding monks, "Monks, do you really believe that Anuruddha caused all this food to be brought"?

"Yes, Venerable Sir", they said.

"Monks, my son Anuruddha does not talk in the way you suggest. Indeed, the canker-free ones never waste their breath on matters like the requisites. The truth is that this alms-offering has been entirely inspired by the supernatural influence of a goddess." And, thereafter, the Tathāgata pronounced this verse:

He whose cankers are destroyed,
Who is no longer bound by food,
Who only resorts to that spiritual deliverance,
The void and the unconditioned Nibbāna:
His path is untraceable,
Like that of birds in the air.

There are several points of great practical importance which arise from this incident, leading to the proclamation of the verse by the Master. It should be noted that excellence invariably attracts opposite reactions, one favouring and the other disfavouring. It also attracts assistance and interest from supernatural sources. Contrarily, *āsavas* attract difficulties and misfortunes.

The goddess, and like her, many other gods and goddesses, including Sakka, the king of the gods, *Devarāja*, were most anxious to serve and adore the saint Anuruddha. Of course, there were also detractors whose distorted perceptions, rooted in the *āsavas*, caused the ugly incident already mentioned.

In a dichotomous world such duality is to be expected. The important fact, however, is that the positive is more powerful, more satisfying, and beautiful.

*Āsavas* are powerful in that they keep beings in the thraldom of *saṃsāric* existence. But whosoever has succeeded in identifying the factors that feed the *āsavas*, and then becomes emancipated from them by not being bound and attached to them, acquires a power which is far more potent.

When one is no longer bound to the fourfold *āhāras*, by resorting to the *vimokkhas*, thus becoming canker-free, one becomes liberated from *saṃsāra*. The canker-free leaves no trace of those factors that keep on laying the track ahead, so as to trap one in the process of drifting endlessly. One becomes, like the bird in the air, untraceable in *saṃsāra*, having achieved a breakthrough into Nibbāna.

# Chapter 5

# Dark And Bright Paths

It is often made out that the question of good and bad is notional, that in reality the so-called good or bad does not exist. That is to say, right and wrong, good and bad are concepts having conventional validity and do not possess ultimate content.

Nothing can be further from the truth, for, if there were no such things as good or bad *per se,* in an absolute sense, there would be no such thing in the world as misery or happiness, poverty or prosperity, beauty or ugliness, disease or health. The inequalities one finds in the world only express the truth of moral causation called *kamma* in Buddhism. And morality means the principle and practices connected with good and bad.

The Buddha was forthright on this point. He cut at the very roots of all ambiguities that prevailed in his time on matters connected with ethics. He emphasized that there are two distinct and mutually opposed ways, *viz.* the dark path and the bright path.

These are not notional paths, nor are they mere concepts or conventions. They are facts, they exist in reality as wholesome and unwholesome mental states, as meritorious and demeritorious actions, happiness and misery, progress and degeneration.

In the Dhammapada, the Buddha succinctly points out
"Abandoning the dark way,
Let the wise cultivate the bright path."

When one rightly and fully understands that ethics and morality deal with absolute values and factors, and that good and bad, right and wrong, wholesome and unwholesome, dark and bright, meritorious and demeritorious are not fictions but actualities, then only is one enabled to understand the mind and its working. For these opposite forces spring from the mind. They are mind-wrought, as it is said in the very first pair of verses in the Dhammapada:

Mind precedes all unwholesome actions
Mind is their chief;
They are all mind-wrought.
If with an impure mind
A person speaks or acts,
Misery follows him
Like the wheel the foot of the drawing ox.

Mind precedes all wholesome actions
Mind is their chief;
They are all mind-wrought.
If with a pure mind
A person speaks or acts,
Happiness follows him
Like his never-departing shadow. (Dhp. 1 and 2)

It is only after having arisen in the mind that they get crystallized as two distinct action-patterns, known in Buddhism as wholesome and unwholesome courses of action—*kusala* and *akusala kammapatha.* Spiritual life, and for that matter all attempts aimed at achieving excellence, begin on one hand with the giving up of the dark ways, and on the other with the cultivation of the bright ways.

And why? Because in the dark ways dwell, and lurk the *āsavas.* And in the bright path are enshrined the factors leading to enlightenment. The dark breeds all that is ill, while the bright is the harbinger of the good. The unwholesome forbodes misfortunes and sufferings, while the wholesome is the repository of good fortune and happiness. The dark is the haunt of turmoil and the bright is the haven of peace. Many such more imageries could be adduced.

Apart from being the cavern of the cankers, the dark bodes ill in a manner more ominous. For, in the darkness lie in ambush portents of evil that threaten holy life in particular. These are known as *cariyā paṭipakkhas*, factors that imperil spiritual life. Basically they are the *āsavas* in dormant form and are identified by the expressive term *upaddava*—potential danger. Whosoever is committed to the one goal of destruction of *āsavas*, which results in the canker-freed state, for him anything that imperils spiritual endeavour is a very serious matter which should forthwith be eradicated.

This is how five hundred monks whose spiritual lives were threatened by a certain *upaddava,* had the great good fortune of availing the Buddha's timely intervention, which led to their deliverance from the dark forces of the *āsavas.* It seems that these five hundred monks, having completed their three-month Rain's Retreat in the kingdom of Kosala, decided to pay their homage to the Blessed One. Accordingly, they went to the Buddha at the Jetavana Monastery at Sāvatthi and prostrating before him respectfully sat down on a side.

Focusing his penetrating mind, the Buddha discerned certain obstacles which lay dormant in their minds, and which, as a potential misfortune, will threaten their holy life in the future. The Blessed One also foresaw what misery could befall them unless he intervened in time and helped them out in the manner of a great surgeon who intervenes before a tumour turns into an irreversible malignant growth.

The Buddha then gave a discourse in keeping with their needs. He led them mentally, step by step, to that ineffable canker-free state where all cankers, potential and active, die a natural death, having nothing to feed on. At the conclusion of the discourse, in order to unfold a step-by-step practical method of advancement, and having the good of posterity in view, the Lord pronounced these verses:

Abandoning the dark way
Let the wise cultivate the bright path,
Going out from home to homelessness—
Detached a joy so rare:
Let him therein alone rejoice.
Giving up sensual pleasures,
With no attachment,
Let the wise man cleanse
Himself of his mental defilements.
Those whose minds have
The fullest excellence reached
In factors of enlightenment,
Who acquisitiveness have renounced,
Who rejoice in not clinging to things:
Having got rid of cankers,
And glowing with wisdom,
They awake into Nibbāna
Even in this very life!

# Chapter 6

## Struggle

Struggle is the salt of life. It is one of those inevitabilities without which nothing can move either for ill or for good. Struggle therefore is the very essence of existence. But then, there are struggles and struggles.

People who toil to amass wealth or to acquire influence, fame and power, or to remain entrenched in position and status, or even to eke out a morsel of food just to exist, invariably have to struggle. And people who do just the opposite, namely, to purge their minds of all evil, to outgrow sensuality to achieve spiritual excellence and self-mastery, they too unavoidably have to struggle. But then, between these two modes of struggle there is a world of difference, a qualitative distinction.

It is therefore absolutely necessary for all seekers of truth to understand that the path to spiritual deliverance is a toilsome path, though a toil that relieves all toil, not that which leads to further toil and prolongs misery. This fact too, has been forcefully pointed out in the *Dhammapada*. It is particularly true of those who discipline themselves vigilantly, intent only upon Nibbāna, so that their cankers fade away.

It appears that in the city of Rājagaha a certain bonded maidservant, Puṇṇā by name, was given by her millionaire master a cruelly strugglesome task, that also led her to freedom from all struggle. In a dichotomous world, what is an impediment only breeds further impediments. But given the wisdom, it can be turned into an aid.

Like the proverbial sword, sharp on both edges, which

can, given the skill, both kill an enemy, and also oneself when ineptly wielded. Every situation in life has two possibilities. A spiritual aspirant, fully comprehending this truth, should so turn all life-situations, even the worst and most miserable ones, to achieve destruction of cankers and therewith saṃsāric bondage. Puṇṇā's bondage was both excruciatingly physical, as well as mental, in the form of doubts, misgivings, being inadequate and inferior etc.

One day, Puṇṇā was given a huge amount of paddy to be pounded into rice. Perspiring and weary, she pounded away until late in the night, with the help of an oil lamp. In order to rest for a while she came outside and stood in the wind. With her body wet with sweat, and struggle writ all over her, she was weighed down with the misery that the *āsavas* of her past actions had wrought on her.

Now, in that brightly moonlit night, she suddenly looked towards the ranges of hills that encircled the city of Rājagaha. And, lo! there was an amazing scene. She saw a procession of monks behind a dignified saintly figure, whose finger was lit, illuminating the whole path for the others. This venerable torch-bearer, his finger acting as a torch by his supernormal attainments, was no other than the legendary saint, the Elder Dabbamallaputta, one of the pre-eminent disciples of the Buddha. He was engaged in showing the large number of monks their individual cells and caves dotting that entire range.

She wondered: "Well, I cannot sleep, even at this hour, weighed down as I am by my misery. But pray, what could be the reason for those happy, free, holy monks not to be resting even now?" Then she found her own logic and surmised, "It must be that some monk is sick, or maybe he is in agony, being bitten by a snake."

Early next morning as she prepared to go to the bathing ghat for her usual wash, she made a coarse *roṭi* (flat bread) out of the pounded red rice powder and tucking it in the fold of her dress, she picked up her water pot and made her way towards the bathing ghat. What transpired on the way was an extraordinary experience that transformed her toil-torn life into one where all toils came to an end.

Now, exactly at that time, the Buddha too deliberately set out on the same path on his alms-round. He had foreseen the outcome of the event how Puṇṇā, the maidservant, would be spiritually transformed.

Meeting the Buddha on the way, Puṇṇā thought, "oh, how wonderful! On other days, whenever I had the good fortune of seeing the Lord, I never had anything to offer or, whenever I had something to offer, I never saw the Lord; but today I do have something to offer and I am also meeting the Lord face to face. If the Buddha were to accept my food without considering whether it is coarse or fine, I would very much like to offer my rice-*roṭi* to him."

So casting down her water pot on one side of the road, she bowed down to worship him and said, "Most Venerable Sir, kindly bestow your blessings on me by accepting this coarse alms-offering."

The Buddha looked at Venerable Ānanda who accompanied him and, receiving a bowl from him, accepted the bonded maid's coarse rice-*roṭi*. After offering the *roṭi* devoutly, Puṇṇā worshipped the Lord again and said, "Most venerable Sir, may the truth, which the Lord himself has realized, be accessible to me also."

"So be it'' said the Blessed One, consecrating her remarkable spiritual act.

Soon, however, Puṇṇā's mind was puzzled as she thought, "though the Lord has bestowed his blessings upon me by accepting my coarse *roṭi*, yet he will not eat this food. On the way definitely he will give it to a crow or a dog, and then going to thc palace of the king or a prince he will partake of a choice meal."

The Buddha discerning her misgivings, looked at Ānanda, signifying his intention to sit down, The Venerable elder spread out a seat and the Lord, sitting on the open road-side, though unusual under normal circumstances, ate the maid's offering. Puṇṇā was moved. After the meal was over, the Buddha put this question to her, "Why did you mistake my disciples?"

"I did not mistake, most venerable Sir."

"Then, what did you say to yourself last night?"

"Most venerable Sir, this is what I thought, 'Well, I cannot sleep even at this hour, weighed down as I am with my own misery. But what could be the reason for these Venerable Ones not to be resting even now? It must be that some monk is sick, or that someone is suffering from snake bite.'"

After hearing her, the Buddha said to her, "Puṇṇā, in your case, you cannot sleep because you are weighed down by your own misery. But in the case of my disciples, they do not sleep because they are unrelentingly exerting themselves for spiritual deliverance. And thereafter, in conclusion, the Lord proclaimed this verse:

"They who are ever vigilant,
Who discipline themselves day and night,
Who are intent only upon Nibbāna
Their cankers fade away." (*Dhp*. 226)

It was indeed remarkable for a poor struggling maid-servant to have sought truth rather than worldly boon in one form or another. Obviously she had a store of spiritual merit which gave her the opportunity to offer such an alms food. The *āsavas*, however, notwithstanding the spiritual potential, did imperil her development. But, by the timely intervention of the Buddha, when the obstacle of doubt was removed, she became spiritually transformed.

# Chapter 7

## Self-important and Heedless

Blindness is a bane and a burden, and mental blindness even more so. Of the many forms of mental blindness, delusion is most insidious, persistent and capricious. And delusion is characterized by pomposity, self-importance, and heedlessness. The heedless is ever negligent, and therefore lacks rectitude and conscience. The self-important man, living in a makeshift world of false values too, lacks mindfulness and moral shame and fear.

Just as the moth is consumed by the flame to which it is attracted by a consuming greed, even so the self-important and the heedless, by neglecting their moral and spiritual responsibilities, and by their cynical, obstinate and callous disregard of principles and values, are consumed by their own egoistic propensity and delusion.

Cheek and vulgarity cannot but aggravate the cankers. It seems some monks living in a township called Bhaddiya lived rather a shameless and worldly life. Though they were committed to the life of frugality and renunciation, to purity and modesty, they were given to most unseemly conduct. They indulged themselves in pursuits which were diametrically opposed to thc spirit and letter of holy life. For instance, they developed a fondness for a foppish lifestyle and behaved like dandies.

It seems these worldly monks used to indulge in making or getting made their sandals and slippers in various styles with elaborate, decorative, ornamental patterns. Even the materials they used—like a special type of grass or rush, palm leaves, lotus stem, reed, wool, etc. were equally exotic and unmonk-like. With their scandalous life-style they greatly embarrassed the good monks. Not only did they tarnish their own minds, but they tarnished the reputation of the holy life itself.

When the matter was reported to the Buddha, who happened to be staying at the Jātiya grove on the outskirts of Bhaddiya, he had these monks assembled and rebuked saying, "Monks, you have taken to holy life for a higher purpose, but now contrary to your calling you are indulging in worldliness." Thereafter he proclaimed these verses:

"What should be done is left undone,
But what should not be done is done;
The self-important and the heedless,
For them the cankers only increase.
Whoso earnestly practise the meditation
On the true nature of the body,
They do not do what should not be done,
They steadfastly pursue what should be done,
For these mindful and clearly comprehending ones,
The cankers do come to an end."

(*Dhp.* 292-3.)

# Chapter 8

## Resting on Laurels

Of all the masquerades that the cankers don, perhaps complacency and smugness can be rated as the most alluring and entrapping. To put on the air of excellence, to be over-confident of one's capacities, to be self-satisfied before the goal is reached, smacks of spiritual smugness and snobbery.

The Buddha never encouraged such self-deceptions. On the contrary, the monks were constantly urged and stimulated by him to reach the canker-free state, and until then never to rest on their laurels.

It is documented that some monks who were well-known for their virtue and other attainments, but who had not yet reached Arahathood, though they were quite confident that they could become Arahats any moment they wished, went to the Buddha at Jetavana, and worshipped him. Discerning their complacent mental states the Lord asked them with a wise and compassionate deliberateness, "Well, monks, have you succeeded in bringing to consummation the spiritual obligation of your holy life?"

They replied individually, some saying, "Most venerable Sir, we have achieved the acme of virtue"; others said, "We have perfected the ascetic practices;" some others "We are very learned;" yet some, "We live a solitary life in remote hermitages"; and some others, "We have attained the meditative absorptions"; some who had become Non-Returners, *(Anāgāmis),* even said, "For us, now, Arahathood is no longer a difficult matter."

And all of them unanimously said, "For us it is not at all difficult to attain the supramundane state of the Perfect One. Indeed, we can attain to Arahathood any day we choose."

On hearing this, the Buddha told them very clearly and firmly, "Monks, merely by achieving purification of morality etc., or even by achieving the bliss born of the supramundane attainment of the high state of the *Anāgāmin*, a monk should never say, "After all, there is but very little worldly suffering left for us. "So long as you have not reached the goal of the destruction of cankers, so long you ought never to allow the thought, 'I am blissful' to arise in you." Thereafter the Buddha pronounced these verses:

"Not by mere rules and observances,
Nor yet by much learning,
Neither by attaining the absorptions,
Nor yet by a life of seclusion,
Nor by thinking 'I enjoy
The bliss of release resorted to by the saints,'
Should you, monks, rest on your laurels
Till you reach
That state void of cankers."

(*Dhp.* 271-72)

# Chapter 9

## Fault-Finding

Fault-finding mirrors one's own mind. A mirror reflects objects, and fault-finding reflects one's own traits. There is no flaw which damages one's character and aggravates one's mental wound, (*āsavas)*, more than the habit of fault-finding.

Fault-finding is a syndrome. It reflects a number of symptoms, complicating the *āsava*-malady even more. Self-righteousness or the holier-than-thou-approach can be at the bottom of fault-finding. Resentment, taking umbrage, malevolence—these hate-rooted factors can give rise to fault-finding. Deceitfulness, cunning, trickery, duplicity, conspiracy, deception or fraudulence—all these can disguise as fault-finding. Sophistry, hypocrisy, misrepresentation, back-biting—these can be at the root of fault-finding. Intolerance, bigotry, dogmatism —these may masquerade as fault-finding. Many more mind defiling factors that the *āsavas* rapaciously feed on could be at the bottom of fault-finding.

It has been mentioned already that, of the three roots of evil, while greed and delusion are cankers, hatred is not. But fault-finding, as a form of hatred, is a rich input that fertilizes the cankers. That is why the Buddha was most emphatic in discouraging the fault-finding tendency, the habit of raising petty objections to every little thing, the censorious air of superiority and virtue.

Yet, correcting somebody out of concern for his or her well-being, which also amounts to pointing out the flaw, has been praised by the Buddha. If a person wants to remove a defect, a lapse or blemish, nothing can be more praiseworthy. Imperfections and failings can be set right only by diligently and lovingly identifying showing them. After all, there is no point in perpetuating a shortcoming.

Therefore, he who finds something that is wrong, unsound and deficient in us uncovers for us a great secret and reveals a real truth. He discloses the secret of success and reveals the truth of perfection. Then, who else can be a better well-wisher? Hence it has been rightly said that one who points out one's faults is a *kalyāṇa-mitta*, a true friend. One of the greatest blessings of life is to have the association of a wise man, who is the true *kalyāṇa-mitta*. Says the *Dhammapada* in the chapter on the wise (*Paṇḍita-vagga*),

"Should you find one who points out faults,
As though indicating a hidden treasure,
Follow such a sagacious man,
A wise person who corrects you;
It is always better and never worse,
To cultivate such an association.

Let him admonish and instruct,
And let him shield you from evil,
He indeed is dear to the good,
Though he be detestable to the evil.

Do not associate with evil companions,
Do not seek the fellowship of the vile,
Associate with true friends,
Seek the fellowship of noble men."

Dhp. 76–78.

It needs circumspection and a perceptive mind to distinguish between a fault-finder and a corrector. In order that one may be endowed with such perspicacious understanding, the Buddha gave a clear call to the monks who had gone to him, much troubled by a rather self-righteous elder, nicknamed the "fault-finder".

It is recorded in the *Dhammapada* Commentary that this monk used to go about finding faults of others, saying, "Look at how this one wears his under-robe, and how he wears his upper-robe!" For every little thing he would find a hole, in season and out of season. So, when it became too much for the fellow-monks to bear the darts of pious air from this 'holy' brother, they went to the Lord so that he might be cured of his disease.

After hearing them, the Buddha said, "Monks, if one who strictly practises the rules of holy life, and who, in order to instruct others, were to point out faults, then it does not amount to fault-finding. But if one, out of a censorious proclivity, goes about finding faults like this monk, for the sole purpose of seeking holes in others, such a person never achieves the ecstatic meditative absorptions and supernormal attainments. For such the cankers only grow. Thereafter, in conclusion, the Blessed One pronounced this verse,

"He who seeks others' faults,
Who is ever censorious,
His cankers only grow;
He is far from destroying cankers."

Dhp. 253.

It would appear that the mark of modernity is generally critical. Fault-finding, in the guise of being critical, is very much in the air. It is the bugbear of modern life.

To be 'critical' is to 'see holes' even if there are none. Various modern democratic methods and practices unabashedly breed devaluation and distrust. Before and during elections, brothers sling mud at brothers, fathers at sons, wives at husbands and *vice versa*.

Character assassinations in public propaganda, abuses in the press and the abounding acerbity in the legislatures, the cinema-violence that provokes vandalism and crime outside, the over-competitiveness of a growing industrial society, the discontent born of unemployment and social disequilibrium, the youth unrest—all these glorified forms of hatred have become concomitants of sophistication and smart human relationship.

The quality of being well-disposed is a *sine-qua-non* for the preservation of culture and higher values and modernism with its fault-finding mania negates this vital quality. From the stand-point of Buddhism, the psychology of fault-finding can be defined as being a projection of one's own limitations. Just as 'want' arises from 'wanting', so also 'seeing faults' arises from 'having faults'. A man is said to be in want when he wants something; similarly, only when a man has some fault within himself can he see faults in others. This summarizes the mechanism of projection which is to say, projecting one's own fault on somebody else. For, seeing it in oneself would be hurting one's ego, and the egoist that the fault-finder is, he just cannot afford to do that.

The fault-finder is characterised by irritability. To be irritable is to be angry with oneself which is expressed in various guises—indignation, disapproval, intolerance of wrong or temper incited by someone's evil. The self-reproach which fault–finding causes amply proves an inner conflict and disharmony.

In Buddhist psychology a sense of guilt manifesting as fault-finding signifies a displacement within the fault-finder, which is tantamount to transferring one's unpleasant impulses or feelings on someone else. This substitution-act or mental displacement only creates blocs within and obstructs spiritual progress. When a portion of a hill slides down or caves in, it blocks the road and disrupts the traffic; even so it is with fault-finding.

# PART II

## Chapter 10

## DESTRUCTION OF CANKERS

He who has destroyed his cankers
Who no longer is bound by the process
Of feeding the body, mind, kammas and rebirths,
Who only resorts to that spiritual deliverance,
Called the unconditioned and the void
Of selfhood and individual existence,
His path is untraceable
Like that of birds in the air.

Dhp.–93.

The goal of Buddhism is the expurgation of mental cankers (*āsavas*), and the path leading to it is a progressive riddance. That is why the one who is freed from cankers is called the Perfect One, the Arahat, the liberated saint.

The destruction of cankers is brought about in three distinct stages or modes, namely, the dormant, the activated and the manifested. This is achieved by the three-pronged operation of *sīla* (purification of morality), *samādhi* (purification of mind) and *paññā* (purification of insight), otherwise known as the Noble Eightfold Path. The logic of this method of destruction is found in the discourse known as *Sabbāsava Sutta*, "Discourse on all Cankers" in the *M. Nikāya*. It consists of the following four points

i. The task.
ii. The individual to fulfil the task.
iii. The rationale.
iv. The methods of overcoming.

It was while staying at Jetavana near the city of Sāvatthi, the capital of the empire of Mahākosala, that the Blessed One enunciated the techniques of overcoming all cankers (*sabbāsava-saṃvara-pariyāya*). This *Sutta* essentially is a practical application of the Noble Eightfold Path, rather than a doctrinal declaration, to enable the followers to outgrow a congenital ailment. It is very typical of the Buddha to evolve practical methods rather than impose commandments and doctrines.

The word *āsava* is an operative term in the dispensation of the Buddha. For, *āsava*-riddance is coexistent with the attainment of Arahathood. It is said in the *Mahāsaccaka Sutta* as well as in the Vinaya, that with the attainment of *āsavakkhaya-ñāṇa*, the future Buddha reached the summit of spiritual attainment, Bodhi. A liberated saint is given the appellation *khiṇāsava*, (the canker-free one), distinctly showing what he has achieved in the form of uprooting inborn disabilities.

An *āsava* is a mental effluent which, arising from the mind, debilitates, defiles and injures it, in the same way rust arising from iron destroys it. An effluent from a factory affects the area in which it is situated by depositing layers of noxious chemicals, and if drained into a river, the whole water-way becomes polluted. The formation of an *āsava* from a dormant state to that of a strong mental current, further crystallised into bodily and verbal actions, constitutes the whole story of bondage in *saṃsāra*, phenomenal existence. All that the Buddha has taught is to nullify these mental effluents *(āsava)* by means of *sīla* (virtue), *samādhi* (meditative concentration) and *paññā* (wisdom).

In the last analysis, the one meaningful goal of spiritual life can only be the achievement of that perfect state where all the cankers have ceased once and for all. The canker-free state indisputably is the ultimate ideal of excellence. Thus the goal as well as the path leading to it are made so explicit here.

Just as from an ulcer loathesome matter oozes out, even so, from an ulcerous mind vicious mental corruptions ooze out through the six sense-doors, the sixth being mind itself.

Just as the banana flower grows out of the banana plant only to kill it, even so, the canker, growing out of the mind, eats into it, weakens it and impairs the moral and spiritual qualities co-existing with it.

Just as a person under the influence of liquor loses mental balance and commits crimes, even against his dearest ones, even so a person under the influence of *āsava* commits all evil deeds. All ethical sense, propriety, moral shame and fear are thrown to the winds and one acts in a way detrimental to both one's own and other's well-being.

In the *Dhammapada* it is said that the Arahat becomes untraceable; he is trackless because he has destroyed the *āsavas*. In other words, *āsava* keeps laying the course upon which a being wanders endlessly in *saṃsāra*. Just as a group of workers would lay a track or path for vehicles or human beings to move on, even so the *āsavas* create a mental track whereby one helplessly commits all kinds of *kammas*–volitional actions, thus projecting oneself into the future.

"Conditioned by cravings there arises clinging, conditioned by clinging there arises becoming, conditioned by becoming there arises birth" said the all-seeing Buddha.

Craving is that mental urge or drive which is characterised by pleasure-seeking, acquisitiveness, the survival instinct and the suicidal psychosis. In our day-to-day life we encounter cravings in the form of lust or greed, egotism, passion, hatred, jealousy, meanness and a variety of other aberrations. At the deepest level this defiling drive exists in the form of an innate tendency known as *anusaya*, the dormant defilement. The idea of oozing or efflux, is synonymous with the lengthening of *saṃsāric* existence and the suffering inherent in it. If the laying of a track is a subjective process, the destruction of it necessarily must be a subjective process as well. It can only be achieved by one's own efforts, commitment and skill.

The *Sutta* enunciates three *āsavas*, namely, the canker of sensual desire (*kāmāsava*), the canker of continued becoming (*bhavāsava*) and the canker of ignorance (*avijjāsava*). The Abhidhamma adds a fourth canker, that of wrong views and ideologies (*diṭṭhāsava*), which the Sutta lists under *bhavāsava.*

The hankering after sensual pleasures in manifold ways, the craze for enjoyment derived through the six sense-doors (i e., the delectable sight, sound, smell, taste, touch, and idea), the drive for the satisfaction of a craving—all these constitute the first category of canker, known as *kāmāsava*.

Self-preservation, the struggle to exist, or that insatiable, craving in the form of clinging to life, the survival instinct, is called 'the canker of becoming' or 'continued existence.' Even an old person of hundred years would seek to continue to live. It would not strike him that he has had a long innings. The blind force to increase bank balances and to cling to power, the urge for possessions—all these are the various tributaries feeding the river of *bhavāsava*.

The man who hoards, increases his possessions or keeps on acquiring more and more money in the fond hope that these will bring him security, misses the fundamental truth that life itself is impermanent. The instinct for survival and security is an expression of this blind urge to continue in spite of impermanence. *Bhavāsava* in this way is complementary to *kāmāsava*, in the sense that it provides the basic structure, namely, rebirth in a particular plane of existence, wherein the urge for pleasure can find fruition.

A man who has fed his senses with pleasurable objects all his life, necessarily creates within himself a psychological condition known as *kamma-sāmaggī,* a combination of kammic forces, which can become effective only when he is reborn again in a realm where the six senses exist. Thus, *bhavāsava* feeds the six senses by causing rebirth, and *kāmāsava* keeps them operating.

Belief has a highly pervasive influence in the life of man because it is that which endows him with a certain attitude, outlook or approach to life. It is the glass through which he sees everything in a certain manner. When this belief or ideology becomes perverse due to its basic falsification and distortion, the mind becomes completely vitiated and therewith the conduct and actions as well.

Rivers of blood have flown on earth in the name of belief. Brothers have fought brothers, people belonging to the same community, religion or race have bitterly hated each other, wiped out each other, all in the name of belief. Harbouring animosity and suspicion, Catholics and Protestants have killed each other through centuries, all in the name of belief, though both happen to be Christians. The various sects among Hindus, Muslims and others have harboured mutual rancour and mistrust, all in the name of belief.

In India, Hindus and Muslims have fought for at least a thousand years, yet the mutual distrust and ill-will continue to erupt every now and then in the form of communal riots. The white man and the black man, the different brands of political, social and economic theories and beliefs are all ideological idiosyncrasies wreaking havoc on mankind.

Whether it is the religious, the materialistic or the agnostic or whatever may be the label, mankind is possessed by the ghost of ideological canker (*diṭṭhāsava*). Wisdom alone can exorcise this ghost. Pride and prejudice, dogmatism and fanaticism, intolerance and bigotry, are the weapons which ideology wields to the detriment of civilization and culture. A broad-minded outlook and objectivity born of wisdom can counter *diṭṭhāsava*, just as detachment and equanimity nullify *bhavāsava*, and dispassion and contentment cancel *kāmāsava*.

Of all cankers, it is said, the canker of ignorance (*avijjāsava*) is the worst. It is the most insidious and tenacious of cankers. Therefore it is called the matrix of all evil. Not only is ignorance 'not knowing', but also knowing perversely and deludedly. It is the canker of ignorance which makes evil appear good, the changeful changeless, the ugly beautiful, the painful pleasant, and the unsatisfactory satisfactory. Since it is both abysmal and pervasive, it produces the illusion of permanence etc., and thereby keeps a being in perpetual bondage. It is through the machinations of the canker of ignorance that man remains 'blissfully' ignorant of the painful realities of *saṃsāra*.

Groping in the pervading gloom of ignorance, man is led to do exactly that which in the light of wisdom he would abhor. Cruelty is more pronounced in a hospital, where compassion should be the ruling influence. Perception of good looks in the body misleads both men and women, where beauty lies in the purity of human mind. Pride misleads the learned, where humility alone adorns knowledge. Hence the saying,

*"Unchastity is the taint in woman,*
*Niggardliness is the taint in a giver:*
*Taints, indeed, are all evil things,*
*Both in this world and in the next.*

*"A worse taint than these is ignorance,*
*The worst of all taints:*
*Destroy this one taint,*
*And become taintless, bhikkhus."*

*Dhammapada*–242-243

The taints corrupt or infect an object. Ignorance thus infects the moral fibre and debilitates the mind in a way that makes it mistake the wrong to be right and *vice versa*. This distortion of actuality is known in Pāli as *vipallāsa*, seeing things topsy-turvy—the impermanent as permanent, pain as pleasure, the non-self or impersonality as the self, the repulsive as attractive etc. From this distorted viewing arises wrong thinking leading to various unwholesome acts—killing, stealing, sexual misconduct, lying, drinking etc. At the moment of death these crystallize into what may be called a "*kamma*-warhead" which, like a nuclear warhead in a rocket, booms into a new state of painful existence.

This brings us to an analysis of the *Sutta* with its fourfold points already mentioned:—the task, the individual to fulfil the task, the rationale and the methods of overcoming. The Buddha makes an exceedingly forthright observation at the very commencement of the *Sutta*.

The Blessed One has said, "Monks, I shall now expound to you the method called the 'control (=overcoming) of all cankers.' Listen and consider carefully, I shall now enunciate." "Yes, most venerable Sir," the monks replied and the Blessed One spoke thus:

"Only for him who understands, who comprehends is there the destruction of cankers, do I say; not for him who does not understand, who does not comprehend. And monks, understanding what, comprehending what, is there the destruction of cankers, do I say? There is the wise consideration and there is the unwise consideration. Monks, for one who unwisely considers, the unarisen cankers arise, and the arisen cankers increase; and, monks, for one who wisely considers, the unarisen cankers do not arise and the arisen cankers are overcome.

*"Monks, there are cankers to be overcome by Insight.*
*There are cankers to be overcome by Self-restraint.*
*There are cankers to be overcome by Judicious Use.*
*There are cankers to be overcome by Endurance.*
*There are cankers to be overcome by Avoidance.*
*There are cankers to be overcome by Elimination.*
*There are cankers to be overcome by Development."*

The most important aspect of this teaching is emphasis on: (a) commitment to an ideal or goal, and (b) an unrelenting endeavour on the part of the committed individual to approximate this goal by orienting the mind to adhere to a wholesome thought-pattern.

The rationale and the methodology concerned with the achievement of the goal are entirely pragmatic, i.e., verifiable in terms of relevance and result, so that the whole procedure or the system is cleared of any dogma, irrationality, blind approach, and superstitious adherence.

As aforesaid the goal is the destruction of cankers, the means are the application of seven distinct methods. These have been so designed by the Buddha so as to suit every possible circumstance and all types of individuals at different levels of spiritual development.

The Blessed One enunciates that it is for "him who understands, who comprehends", that there is the destruction of cankers, "not for him who does not understand, does not comprehend", that is, does not see things as they really are. The Four Noble Truths are implied here by the terms understanding and comprehending. In other words, it is only for a seeker who in his day-to-day life comprehends the validity of the Four Noble Truths that wise consideration becomes natural. Understanding is like the fulcrum on which is placed the lever of wise consideration, to lift the mind to a higher dimension of awareness, leading to the destruction of cankers.

The Four Noble Truths are not theories, but insightful intuitive experiences during meditation. In the dispensation of the Buddha, a serious aspirant practising the *vipassanā* meditation actually experiences these truths, in the same way a man with the senses intact would see an object, hear music, smell the fragrance of a flower, taste a good meal or come in touch with the cool breeze on a hot day.

*Āsavas* cannot be even contained, much less destroyed, by mere knowledge. For, cankers lie deeper than intellect can fathom. Only by intuitive wisdom supported by virtue and mental purity can these be overcome. Knowledge is manifold, emphasised Ācariya Buddhaghosa in the *Visuddhi-magga*. Continuing, said the Ācariya, "in the dispensation of the Buddha a monk who misuses medical knowledge by practising medicine, which is not the proper vocation for a Buddhist monk, in him through such knowledge, the *āsavas* only grow. Therefore, what is intended here is that comprehension of truth based on wise consideration which destroys the *āsavas*."

In this *Sutta* the key term is 'wise consideration' *(yoniso manasikāra)*, which is characterised by a definite psychological outcome. "For one who unwisely considers, the unarisen cankers arise, and the arisen cankers increase, i.e. get further strengthened. For one who wisely considers, the unarisen cankers do not arise and the arisen cankers are overcome."

When a person indulges in unwholesome thinking, the dormant *āsavas* become activated and the activated ones get further vitalised. Similarly, when one reflects in a wise way and comprehends things as they really are, the dormant *āsavas*, not being activated, die of atrophy, and the activated *āsavas* are overcome. From the standpoint of psychology this teaching of the Buddha has a tremendous significance. The whole mechanism of the development of mind and the unfolding of the spiritual potential rest on this premise.

Wise consideration is pivotal. It is like the hub around which revolves the entire methodization for the overcoming of *āsavas*. What is emphasized is to give right direction to mental activities. It is like fitting an engine on an armed tank or an ambulance. The resultant destruction or saving of life is entirely based on which the engine is fitted to. The engine is neutral. It has no choice. How it is used is the concern of those who are dealing with the engine. So it is with *manasikārā*, consideration. As a matter of fact, *manasikāra* is one of those innocuous mental factors (*cetasika*) which is associated with every state of consciousness. That is why it is called a 'primary mental factor,' common to all states *(sabba-citta-sādhāraṇa),* wholesome (*kusala*), unwholesome (*akusala*) and neutral or indeterminate (*avyākata*).

Literally *manasikāra* means *manaṃ karoti*–"makes the mind to attend that," i.e.to consider, direct attention, think etc. In this context *manasikāra,* therefore, is fixing one's mind totally to a certain purpose, having a thorough-going method in one's thought.

The word *yoniso* (wise) is derived from the word *yoni*, which means womb, origin, a matrix, place of birth or realm of existence. Contrarily, *ayoni* (unwise), signifies an ignorant origin, something essentially shallow and muddled. *Yoniso* therefore implies, something wise, proper and 'down to its origin.'

In other words *yoniso manasikāra* means considering things wisely *i.e.* with insight, in the right manner, making wisdom the womb, the source or matrix of one's thinking. In other words, it means purposive and meaningful thinking with a definite goal in view, rooted in insight into reality. When the grass roots of the mental process are healthy and moral, and when spiritual values keep the mind illuminated, the outcome must also be healthy, wholesome and productive of excellence. This is the psychological implication.

Contrarily, by *ayoniso manasikāra* is implied an unwholesome origin, *i.e.* wrong thought, or muddled mental working; but due to its essential superficiality and rootlessness; something which, like cancer, infects and weakens the entire mental structure. Briefly it signifies disorderly and destructive mental activity.

The immense practical implications of these two terms need to be fully grasped. For, on them rests the whole business of bondage in or liberation from *saṃsāra*—worldly existence.

*Yoniso* and *ayoniso* are the two operative principles that determine the validity or non-validity of the seven methods adumbrated in the *Sutta*. *Yoniso* stands for *vivaṭṭa*—becoming un-involved, turning away from or falling out of the wheel of becoming. *Ayoniso*, on the other hand, means being involved, getting more and more caught in the vicious circle otherwise called *vaṭṭa*. So, while the former means disentanglement from mundane existence, the latter means entanglement in it.

*Saṃvaṭṭa* and *vivaṭṭa* are cosmological terms. The former means the dissolution and destruction of the world brought about by the intensity and universal prevalence of the unwholesome and evil factors, while the latter signifies a process of evolution, unfolding and regeneration of the world, bringing about the evolution of beings based upon the prevalence of wholesome factors. From this it is clear that the coming into being or the fading away of the phenomenal world depends upon mental activities that are basically wise or unwise, wholesome or unwholesome.

This brings us to the seven methods, which are effective only when they are powered by wise consideration, like an engine becoming operative when appropriately fuelled. Said the Blessed One:

*"Monks, there are cankers to be overcome by insight,*
*There are cankers to be overcome by self-restraint,*
*There are cankers to be overcome by judicious use,*
*There are cankers to be overcome by endurance,*
*There are cankers to be overcome by avoidance,*
*There are cankers to be overcome by elimination,*
*There are cankers to be overcome by development."*

The first method, that is, 'to be overcome by insight', refers to the cultivation of intuitive insights (*vipassanā-ñāṇa*) into the basic facts or realities of impermanence, unsatisfactoriness and un-substantiality that characterise everything in phenomenal existence, *saṃsāra.* In actual application it means the practice of insight-meditation and therewith cultivating the insightful awareness of the three characteristics. When insight into the characteristics becomes a direct experience, as different from an intellectual one, the mind is freed of all distortions and impurities, and the insights into the Four Noble Truths flash, illuminating the consciousness. This is a very wonderful experience that shakes one's very being, weakening thereby the deep-rooted *āsavas*, attenuating them more and more every-time the flashes of insight occur within. Having developed all the stages of *vipassanā* (insight), as one finally ascends upon the summit of spiritual experience of the supramundane and succeeds in breaking the fetters (*saṃyojana*) that tie one to mundane existence, it is then that the *āsavas* get eradicated once and for all.

The highest supramundane stage known as Arahathood is characteristically called *khiṇāsava*, the canker-freed state. This is the highest state of spiritual excellence and the goal of all spiritual endeavour. The canker-freed saint is the true refuge for all beings in the world. For, he alone, having transcended the *saṃsāric* bondages, can help others to do similarly. Only he who knows can teach, not the one who does not know. And only he who is liberated can help in others' liberation, not those who are still in bondage, however mighty, exalted, talented and fortunate they may be, like the gods (*devas).*

The second method refers to the cultivation of mindfulness and, therewith, self-control and self-mastery. In actual practice, self-mastery means having control over the senses. Control does not mean repressing a sense-faculty or making a given sense-door inoperative. The eye, ear, nose, tongue, body and mind are the six senses, and control over them does not mean stopping them from functioning or manipulating them in an unnatural manner. All that is meant by self-control is being watchful at the sense-doors and thereby having full control over them.

It is like placing a sentry at a gateway or door, who has full control over his area by virtue of his vigilance thereon. Similarly, when a seeker applies mindfulness on any one of the sense-doors, by this simple act of attentiveness or vigilance, all cankers are automatically removed, if they have arisen, and if there are none, the mind is so fortified that they cannot arise.

While eating, if a person is mindful, he cannot overeat, thus he obviates the possibility of the cankers arising and polluting the mind. If a particular visible object or sight, when attended to, is likely to defile the mind, by being mindful at the eye sense-door, that is to say, by being aware of the process of seeing, he will keep at bay the possibility of a canker arising; and if one has arisen, then, by knowing that it has, he will ward it off. Thus, self-control primarily is a mental operation in the form of an alert and attentive awareness that notes and observes everything, leading to the warding off of the unwholesome.

When mindfulness is cultivated through various contemplative exercises formulated by the Buddha, such as the special system known as the *satipaṭṭhāna*, various other factors too are simultaneiously cultivated based on synchronic function. When one finger is pulled, all the five fingers are also pulled; or when a corner of a carpet is pulled, the entire carpet gets pulled. In like manner, when through the various techniques of the *satipaṭṭhāna* meditation, mindfulness is developed, a number of other spiritual factors like mental tranquillity, faith, effort, insight, endurance, sagacity, in fact, all the seven components of Enlightenment or the factors of the Noble Eightfold Path become developed too.

The third method refers to the judicious use of all the requisites or basic needs of life, such as food, clothing. shelter and medicaments. This is done by wisely reflecting on why these necessities are required and how they are to be utilized in the best possible way. Here, the motivating factor is practical wisdom or sagacity. To be sagacious, one should pause and ponder, before and during utilizing any requisites of life, and be heedful.

The fourth method is to consciously and deliberately endure difficulties and afflictions caused by external circumstances, harsh treatment by others, and adversity in general. One can set oneself right, but not always and everywhere. In order that one may face a hostile and disagreeable environment imperturbably, it is essential that one must learn to be patient, forbearing and forgiving. Those who lack fortitude can never make the best use of life, much less overcome cankers. Enduring patience, therefore, has been extolled by the Buddha as one of the most exalted virtues and a spiritual perfection (*pāramī*) which must necessarily be fulfilled if one must attain Nibbāna, the *summum bonum.* Said the Buddha:

*"Enduring patience is the highest austerity,*
*Nibbāna is supreme, so the Buddhas say:*
*Verily, he is not a monk who harms another,*
*Nor is he a recluse who oppresses others."*

Dhp.–184

So long as the canker remains dormant, it may not disturb one much, in the sense that the conscious mind may not be in its grip, or be inundated by its swirling currents. But, once it is activated and allowed to function at the conscious level, it overwhelms the mind and becomes "destructive and consuming", and finds expression in the form of verbal or bodily action. Even at the conscious mental level (*pariyuṭṭhāna*), it is overpowering enough, but when it expresses itself in deed and word, it can be ominous and deadly.

It is said that diseases infect. In fact, a canker, as a destructive mental disease, is far more contagious. It not only affects one, but countless others with whom one comes in contact. That is why the *Sutta* is emphatic that "whatever cankers arise through non-endurance, it becomes destructive and consuming. However, through endurance these cankers, liable to be destructive and consuming, do not arise." Here is a rationale that is incontrovertible and practical.

The fifth method is concerned with external situations and

confrontations which, if not avoided prudently, may become calamitous. Recklessness and thoughtlessness are the twin mental evils that are at the root of most of life's ills and mishaps. Discretion is the better part of valour, it is said, and wisely so. There is nothing heroic about a dare-devil. To be foolhardy is to be a fool.

What is the fun in facing a fierce bull, elephant, snake and the like? Likewise, to be venturesome with respect to resorts and associates known to be dangerous, is certainly a reckless risk. One of the greatest boons in life is to associate with the wise, and, conversely, one of the greatest misfortunes is to get involved with depraved friends. It is like being thrown into a cesspool. The wise thing, therefore, is to avoid such situations which, even in the slightest measure, pose danger to life, physically, mentally and spiritually.

Avoidance should not be understood as a calculative and opportunistic measure for self-preservation. Essentially, it is an ethical response, based on moral fear and moral shame. It means refraining from anything and any situation that may endanger one morally. Just as in the first method, insight into and clear comprehension of the realities of life constitute the core-element of the method of overcoming, in the second, mindfulness, in the third, practical wisdom or sagacity, in the fourth, endurance: in this fifth method, it is virtue or moral purification (*sīla* that constitutes the moving force of the method).

The sixth method is that of elimination of wrong thoughts or urges, such as thoughts of sensual desire, anger, cruelty etc., which, if not done away with, grow into a mighty mental barriers that block all spiritual progress. A wrong thought, as a mental action, is a pollutant, which disrupts totally the ecology of the mind. It is therefore imperative that as soon as an unwholesome thought arises, it should be liquidated forthwith. This means a vigorous and energetic mental application, called Right Effort.

The primary function of effort is to keep at bay any unwholesome mental urge or propensity that has not yet taken a definite shape, as a conscious thought, and if, by some chance, the wrong thought has arisen, to make an end of it. Conversely, Right Effort also means to cultivate wholesome thoughts that have not been cultivated, and to stabilize what has already been cultivated. The main thrust of this method, therefore, means an active and effortful mental commitment.

The seventh method is perhaps the most vital, in that it is aimed at the development of those supremely positive and elevating mental qualities known as Enlightenment Factors. If Enlightenment can be visualized in the form of a body of illuminating experiences, converging upon the transcendent, and thus effecting that glorious linkage of the mundane with the supramundane, then, each of these Enlightenment Factors constitute a separate limb of that illuminating body. Each limb, therefore, has to fulfil a very unique, potent and essential function, the sum-total of which synchronises and blooms into Enlightenment. These Enlightenment Factors are mindfulness, investigation of truth, effort, rapture, tranquillity, meditative concentration, and equanimity.

This method of developing positive spiritual qualities is an all-embracing one. It relates to every thought, word and deed, and therefore amounts to a total involvement in a process that increasingly induces here and now verifiable spiritual excellence. There is nothing nebulous or ambiguous in this mode of spiritual development. One's progress can be measured and clearly identified moment to moment through every transaction of life. In fact, life can be reduced to a given action as its ultimate unit. If this action is spiritually negative, then by the application of this method, it can be forthwith transformed into a positive and purposive spiritual action. Thus the seventh method is the alchemy of turning the base metal of cankers into the gold of spirituality. Through every action, through every deed, word and thought, this can and should be done, without creating the dichotomy of spiritual and secular values, without the false, watertight, compartmentalization of life.

This method comprehends all the thirty-seven requisites of enlightenment known as *bodhipakkhiyā dhammā*. In actual practice it amounts to following the Noble Eightfold Path, or, succinctly put, fulfilling the task of the threefold purification at the moral, mental and insight levels (*sīla*, *samādhi*, *paññā*).

To sum up, if one recapitulates the logic of the *Sutta* in the form of (i) the task, (ii) the individual, (iii) the rationale and (iv) the methods of overcoming, it would be clear that the sole purpose is to overcome cankers, indefatigably, with might and main. The individual who fulfils this undertaking with unreserved commitment, is "the one who understands and comprehends'' the nature of the *āsavas*, the efficacy of wise consideration and the sevenfold methods. Indeed the Buddha did spell clearly the qualification required for this undertaking when he said, "only for him who understands, who comprehends, is there the destruction of cankers, not for him who does not understand, who does not comprehend."

From this statement of the Buddha, it is evident that those who are ambivalent about moral and spiritual matters, who do not believe in the law of moral causation (*kamma*), who are not interested in getting out of *saṃsāric* bondage, and who are in the grip of mental defilements, are not the individuals who can undertake to fulfil this task of overcoming cankers. Unless there is a compelling urge for excellence and a clearcut understanding of the goal and the means, it is just not possible to come to grips with these insidious and ominous inner enemies, the cankers.

The rationale (*yutti*) is the plain pragmatism of *yoniso manasikāra* which says, "For one who unwisely considers, the unarisen cankers arise, and the arisen cankers increase; and, monks, for one who wisely considers, the unarisen cankers do not arise, and the arisen cankers are overcome." The approach, thus, is psychological, as distinct from metaphysical or speculative. It is the practical outcome that matters, and not the niceties of the doctrines and theories, or the fastidiousness of the learned. The manner of working consists of the aforesaid seven methods of overcoming the cankers

The question may be raised that if only the wise men can fulfil the task, and the wise are a microscopic minority, then what about the unwise or not-so-wise who constitute the vast majority? Should they remain unredeemed since the scope of the *Sutta* is specifically limited to the spiritual elite?

When the Buddha specified that it is for "one who understands and comprehends that there is the destruction of cankers", all that is emphasized is the imperative of training and discipline. In the world, where beings are enmeshed in sensuality and delusion, it is hardly possible for them to comprehend that they are indeed enmeshed. A sick man cannot be expected to carry out a task which only a healthy man can do. Similarly, those who are entangled, and who want to remain entangled and have no interest in getting themselves disentangled, they are certainly sick people mentally, and for them to accomplish this task would require appropriate training and discipline. They have to be motivated to undertake this task, and they must re-orient their mental approach so as to enable themselves to fulfil the task. That is all, and this certainly does not mean excluding anybody.

The universality of the message of the Blessed One is further accentuated and never contradicted or diminished by the emphasis that everyone should be helped to understand and comprehend, and not just encouraged to remain blinded by mandatory faith, dogma and commandments.

# Chapter 11

## CANKERS AND DELIVERANCE

Why is it that the *Sabbāsava Sutta* mentions only these three *āsavas,* the cankers of sensual desire, continuation of becoming and ignorance? Reference has been made that the *Abhidhamma* adds one more *āsava*, namely, the canker of wrong views. But this has been already included in the second of the *Sutta* classifications. The canker for the continuation of becoming can arise only when there is an ideological base which confirms becoming, and even extols it.

This threefold classification of cankers has a very profound purpose. It stands directly in opposition to the threefold spiritual deliverance known as *vimokkha*. The *āsavas* are called *vimokkha-paccanīka*, the reverse of deliverance, or the adversaries of deliverance. The three *vimokkhas* are the *animitta vimokkha*, signless deliverance, *appanihita vimokkha*, desireless deliverance and *suññatā vimokkha*, voidness deliverance. These derive their names from the contemplations of the three characteristics namely, contemplation of impermanence—*aniccānupassanā*, contemplation of unsatisfactoriness—*dukkhānupassanā* and contemplation of non-self—*anattānu-passanā.*

No specific or sacrosanct reason need be ascribed to the order so mentioned. The *Paṭisambhidā-magga*, for instance, starts with *anattānupassanā* and *suññatā vimokkha,* which are the last in the aforementioned order. This is also true with reference to the order of the *āsavas* namely, *kāmāsava*, *bhavāsava* and *avijjāsava*—the canker of sensuality, the canker for the continuation of becoming, and the canker of ignorance.

It may be seen from these lists that the canker of sensuality stands diametrically opposed to the 'desireless deliverance,' which arises from the contemplation of unsatisfactoriness. Similarly, the canker of ignorance constitutes the negative counterpart of the 'voidness deliverance,' which stands for the faculty of wisdom, penetrating unsubstantiality or non-self. And the canker for the continuation of existence is the antithesis of 'signless deliverance,' reflecting universal flux, moment to moment change.

The *vimokkhas* are developed only when one has a firm and determined anchorage in the contemplation of the three-fold characteristics (*lakkhaṇas*) that mark everything in the cosmos. These contemplations, in course of time, grow into a perception (*saññā*) and get embedded, as it were, in the consciousness.

*Anicca-saññā*, is the perception of the intrinsic impermanence or changefulness of all phenomena. *Dukkha saññā*, is the perception of the underlying involvement and affliction, the condition of unsatisfactoriness that marks worldly existence. And *anatta saññā,* is the perceptioin of non-self, that is, the impersonal function or unsubstantiality of everything that is. In effect, these perceptions, mean seeing things as they really are, not as they appear to be. When the mind is fully oriented to comprehend according to the three-fold characteristics, this insight into the actuality of things, automatically delivers the mind from the bondage of the cankers.

Sensual desire arises only when one fails to see that whatever is desired, acquired, possessed and hoarded, must unavoidably be lost, because everything is changing. On the contrary, if one is firmly established in the perception of impermanence, the mind automatically acquires the qualities of detachment and dispassion, factors diametrically opposed to desire, possesiveness, lust, passion etc.

The struggle for existence, the survival instinct or what the Buddha calls the craving for and clinging to the continuation of existence, is a canker that arises because of the inability of the mind to discern the universality of involvement and affliction, the pervasive unsatisfactoriness which characterises everything that is impermanent. Whatever is changeful must be lost; and in the loss there is anguish; and anguish is suffering, *dukkha*, as an underlying metaphysical reality. If the mind is oriented and trained to penetrate into the truth of universal unsatisfactoriness, of subjection to pain and suffering, intrinsic in whatever is unpredictable and uncertain, which life is, then the craving for becoming, for the continuation of worldly existence, does fade away.

Ignorance essentially is not knowing, not seeing or refusing to know and see the realities. How pervasive and powerful this mental canker is has been clearly enunciated by the Buddha in his teachings on the Four Noble Truths, which constitute his discovery of the realities. The Four Noble Truths do not form a doctrine or theory but is a meditative experience. These truths have to be actualized by every aspirant seeking to achieve enlightenment. The Pāli Canon very clearly spells out the definition of ignorance as not knowing, not seeing, the truth of universal suffering (*dukkha-sacca*); not knowing not seeing the cause of suffering which is craving (*dukkha-samudaya-sacca*); not knowing, not seeing the cessation of suffering, which is the dimension of freedom, Nibbāna (*dukkha-nirodha-sacca*); not knowing, not seeing, the path that leads to Nibbāna (*dukkha-nirodha-gāmini-paṭipadā-sacca*).

Ignorance not only veils the truths of life, but makes them appear in a topsy-turvy and distorted manner (*vipallāsa*), so that whatever is basically transient appears to be lasting, whatever is innately imperfect, unsatisfactory and suffering, to be perfect, satisfactory and happiness, whatever is unsubstantial, to be substantial and possessed of a self. Similarly, it perversely projects the truth of the ultimate freedom Nibbāna, to be nihilistic, and the path to Nibbāna to be inadequate, thus making out the secure to be insecure.

This distortion of the Truths has many other implications. The mind holds on to perverse views and inclines towards world-affirming *kammas*, justifies worldliness, extols worldly existence to be something worth enjoying, and builds up a proclivity towards permissiveness and clinging. Ignorance, thus, is the root-cause of all evil. It is the mother of all cankers.

Like a 'blackout' ignorance keeps the mind in darkness and blocks the arising of wisdom and all that is beneficial. Like the cloud that covers the sun, it covers actuality. Like the ever-green, thick tropical jungle, where the sun's rays can never penetrate, it banishes one into the murky, damp, inner jungle where a festering mind lets the cankers ooze.

As the canker-causing mental blindness, ignorance signifies not merely the absence of knowledge or comprehension, but the presence of wrong knowledge and perverted understanding. It arises primarily because of an egocentric propensity, which, like the magician's sleight of hand, creates the deception that life, after all, is everlasting, ever-pleasurable and the expression of an everlasting self or soul, an underlying unchangeable entity in a changing world. The sense of 'I', or anything belonging to the 'I', is a fiction or hallucination that ignorance most effectively contrives in collusion with the canker of becoming, the compulsion of survival, to subjugate the mind. Thus, ignorance being primordial and abysmal, feeds and nourishes the other cankers.

When the mind is oriented to see through these fictions, and is enabled to percieve the three characteristics, only then does it remain in the light of wisdom. An illuminated mind can never be stormed by the dark forces of ignorance.

If the *āsavas* hold the mind in a vice-like grip, the perception of the three characteristics releases the mind. They constitute approaches to liberation from bondage, and consequantly the particular type of deliverance arising from each mode of perception is also known as a gateway to deliverance (*vimokkha -mukha*).

Concerning these three gateways to deliverance, the *Paṭisambhidāmagga*, the Path of Analytical Knowledge, very lucidly explains thus: "Whosoever, filled with determination, wisely considers all formations to be impermanent (*anicca*), he attains to the 'signless deliverance,' *animitta-vimokkha*. Whosoever, filled with tranquillity, wisely considers all formations to be affliction or suffering (*dukkha*), he attains to the 'desireless deliverance,' *appaṇihita-vimokkha*. Whosoever, filled with understanding, wisely considers all formations to be non-self or unsubstantial (*anattā*), he attains to the 'voidness deliverance,' *suññata-vimokkha*."

Here 'signless,' *animitta*, means conditionless. Conditions appear in the mind as so many images or signs, *nimittas*, when the mind is in the grip of *kāmāsava*, filled with mental images of all kinds, keeping it distracted and thus in a state of fragmentation.

The perception of impermanence and the resultant detachment reverses this process of the mind being invaded by swarms of signs or images, concepts or ideas, thus enabling one to enjoy a state of freedom from distracting thoughts etc. This is called the 'signless deliverance,' the positive counterpart of the negative *kāmāsava*.

Sensuality is characterised by running after objects, which,like shadows, ever recede, provoking thereby an insatiable thirst and craving and an anguish and affliction from the inevitable non-fulfilment or frustration. On the other hand, the perception of impermanence is characterised by a turning away from things. Hence the appellation 'signless deliverance.'

Here by 'desireless deliverance,' *appaṇīhita-vimokkha*, is to be understood a condition of mind which is not bent towards anything (*appaṇihita*); that is to say, it does not aim at any object or formation and get stuck thereon and be fettered. Thus non-inclination towards getting stuck to anything arises from the determined awareness of suffering. When one discerns that everything is afflicted in some way, naturally there is no inclination to get stuck thereon, which is what desire means.

The canker for continuation of becoming establishes a vicious circle, a synonym of suffering. When one is subjected to recurring becoming (*bhawa*), when one aimlessly and endlessly drifts upon the ocean of *saṃsāra*, inextricably caught in an unpredictable and helpless situation, it produces anguish and suffering. The perception of suffering or affliction naturally does away with any desire to be involved in a vicious circle of suffering and helplessness. This is called 'desireless deliverance.'

Similarly, by the 'voidness deliverance,' *suññatā-vimokkha*, is to be understood that state of consciousness which is freed from the grip of self-illusion and the belief in a permanent entity called 'soul' etc. Metaphysical speculations about self, soul, ego, etc., invariably create perverse ideological and theological dogmas, thus intolerance and bigotry. It is this self-illusion again that is the matrix of all other defilements. I-ness and my-ness constitute the well-spring of greed, passion, hatred, conceit and vanity. Thus, when such a circle of defilements is established, the vicious circles of *kamma* and its corollary rebirth too get established. Such is the insidious and ominous power that lurks in self-illusion.

When one perceives *anatta*, the unsubstantiality intrinsic in everything, the state of being conditioned and the impersonal function of everything, one's mind naturally is released from the grip of self-illusion, and egotism. The mind becomes void (*suñña*) of the illusory notion of selfhood; it is emptied of any ideological or theological preferences. Hence the appellation, 'voidness deliverance.'

Further, the *Paṭisambhidāmagga* provides an elaborate analysis showing how a combination and permutation of the perception of the three *lakkhaṇas* can conduce to all three *vimokkhas*. This is what the insight meditation or *Vipassanā* aims to achieve—the canker-freed state of the Arahat (*khīṇāsava*).

# Chapter 12

## WISDOM IN ACTION

As a practical application, wise consideration is considering things in the light of the basic truths of existence. It means formulating an approach firmly rooted in the fundamentals, that is to say, in the three characteristics of impermanence, suffering and non-self.

When one gets used to viewing things against the backdrop of these three characteristics, one naturally develops a certain perception, otherwise known in Pāli as *anicca-saññā, dukkha-saññā*, and *anatta-saññā* (perceptions of impermanence, unsatisfactoriness and non-self). It is this perception and the skill of its application in a given situation that constitute 'wise consideration.' Thus, wise consideration boils down to just one thing, namely, a certain mental approach necessary to meet a given circumstance in a way that becomes spiritually productive and edifying.

If one looks at life in its broad outlines, one can identify three distinct contexts in which to relate one's approach appropriately.

These are:

i. An approach relating to the working of one's own mind-thoughts, urges compulsions, obsessions, feelings, notions, views, opinions etc.

ii. An approach relating to different individuals—dear ones, friends, neutrals, enemies etc. This can be called an approach regarding inter-personal relationships.'

iii. The approach towards an impersonal situation—the type of work and routines in which one is involved in various places—at home, in a school, factory, office etc.

A discernment of the method best suited to a given situation has been expounded in the *Sabbāsava Sutta* in the form of seven distinct methods. These methods require practical application of wisdom, that is to say, of wise consideration.

The seven methods enunciated by the Buddha are faultless and all-inclusive. They stand out as self-evident facts. For instance, when one is mentally troubled by metaphysical, theological or ideological speculations or thinking, there cannot be a better method than the application of insight (*vipassanā*) relating to the Four Noble Truths, or to the three characteristics of *anicca*, *dukkha* and *anatta*. For, speculation only means a diffused and discursive state of mind. It only reflects unknowing or wrong knowing. Whatever one is not sure of, one speculates about that. This 'not being sure' is the essence of ignorance and delusion. It is like a shadow that darkens the mind.

The only effective method there is the cultivation of insight. When a person speculates about his or her nature, however natural and philosophical it is made out to be, thinking: "Was he, or was he not in the past; what will he be or not be in the future; and what exactly is he, or is he not, in the present?", for sheer sanity, it will be necessary to place the so-called 'I' in the light of the realities of *anicca*, *dukkha* and *anatta*. Forthwith the mind will be disabused of the illusions that speculation creates. Theories, imaginations and assumptions on self, soul, etc. are based on speculative thinking. They are like mental dice-games, depending on chance, not on reality. In a situation when the mind indulges in any form of speculative thinking, the effective way to change this course is to practise wise consideration, which would replace theories etc. by direct experience. Such direct experience of oneself through a foolproof, objective method such as the *vipassanā* meditation would reveal the true nature of 'self' to be something transient, afflicted and unsubstantial.

It is the same with other methods, *viz*. control etc. The six senses can be controlled only by mindfulness, when wise consideration is added to it, and not by manipulation; one's skill to meet the trickiest of situations that mind creates is further heightened thereby. An alert and comprehending mind can successfully overcome the masquerades of self-deceptions, the specious thoughts etc. that arise in the mind, defiling and debilitating it. All evil and unwholesome mental states or conditions can be averted only by constant watchfulness. This is done naturally at the doors of the mind, namely the senses.

The effective method of keeping out thieves from committing burglary is to block the access to the house. The senses provide access to the mind; as an unguarded access door places the house at the mercy of the burglar, similarly when the sense-doors remain unguarded by mindfulness, the mind is ever at the mercy of the defilements. Those who say that one can contain the desires while gratifying the senses, the materialistic approach, are obviously suffering from self-deception. Self-control reflects wise consideration. As such, it is an efficient method devised to deal with oneself. That is to say, to deal with one's mind, with others, and with all situations of life.

Judicious use is the third method that relates to one's needs like food, clothing, medicaments and shelter. It is hardly necessary to emphasise how, by increasing needs or by improper use of needs, one can incarcerate oneself within the prison-house of a corrupt life. People who live beyond their means are generally frustrated and discontented for not having more; they live a life of strife and struggle. This is misery one invites, by going more than half the way, and it can easily be countered by a judicious use of the necessities of life and this calls for wise consideration, the alchemy that turns a wasteful and wayward use into a purposive and profitable one.

The fourth method, endurance, can be described as a superb technique that can face all circumstances, including the most painful ones. There are many situations in life which cannot be tackled in any other way but through forbearance and forgiveness, through enduring patience. Those who tend to be impatient, who cannot bear difficulties in life or endure harsh speech, loss etc., also cannot effectively face success, affluence and honour.

Without a measure of spiritual development it is very difficult to retain the good things with which one is rewarded. That is why one often finds a successful government official becoming haughty and impatient, a politician becoming corrupt and unscrupulous, a businessman becoming avaricious and hypocritical, a doctor, engineer, orator, or a religious leader, a whole society becoming utterly unprincipled and selfish through lack of spiritual commitment. This trend of impatience invariably leads an individual to downfall, and all one's good things of life get lost. Throughout the world such rise and fall of fortune have occurred and are occurring because of the rise and fall of spiritual values and practices.

One should therefore learn to endure even success and fame, as much as failures and miseries, so that one may lead a balanced life of moderation and sobriety. Endurance is an expression of wise consideration. It truly is a powerful weapon that can be devastatingly wielded to meet all challenges.

In meeting a perilous situation or an oncoming danger, a moment's indiscretion or carelessness is enough to deprive one of his or her life or to destroy one's character or career. Only avoidance, born of wise reflection, can save one from such an eventuality. The fifth method of avoidance is therefore eminently practical.

Even so is the sixth method, that of elimination, which is concerned with the elimination of wrong thoughts or mental conditions such as cupidity, anger, cruelty etc. Any unwholesome thought should not be endured, but forthwith eliminated, if one wants to prevent avoidable pain and peril.

Ultimately, thoughts are the wellsprings of one's actions. Actions account for one's conduct and conduct makes what one is. If wrong thoughts are allowed to arise, then one's mind, one's conduct, even one's whole life can become soiled, bringing untold misery in its wake.

The last method, *i.e.,* overcoming cankers by development, should be considered the most vital one for, it brings into existence positive qualities. On the one hand, it does away with all that is unwholesome and evil, and on the other, helps in the flowering of spiritual qualities known as enlightenment-factors. These factors are the components of the exalted supramundane attainment, called 'enlightenment,' which is a crowning of spiritual transformation. With enlightenment, one has a direct vision of Nibbāna, when one cuts asunder the vicious circle of *kamma* and rebirth, and severs the ten fetters that had kept one enchained in phenomenal existence through immeasurable time, and one accomplishes the task of winning the eternal freedom and peace of Nibbāna.

These seven concomitants of enlightenment known as *bojjhaṅgas* (enlightenment factors) are: Mindfulness, Investigation of Truth, Effort, Rapture, Tranquillity, Meditative Concentration and Equanimity. As these *bojjhaṅgas* are "based on detachment, dispassion and cessation" and "mature into abandonment", they are called the factors of enlightenment, brought about by the supramundane path and fruition insights, (*lokuttara-magga* and *phala)*, signifying the transformation of mind. Only when this happens does one transcend worldly attachment, greed, passion, lust, hatred, delusion, ignorance and such other mental fetters that keep one in perpetual bondage to *saṃsāra.*

This exalted attainment can be understood both subjectively and objectively. Subjectively, Nibbāna signifies the cessation of craving, ignorance, and therewith involvement in *kamma.* Objectively, Nibbāna signifies the cessation of recurring existence or rebirth brought about by kamma, and leading to the mass of suffering of worldly existence. According to the *paṭicca samuppāda*, the law of dependent origination, *saṃsāra* represents the three cycles (*vaṭṭa*) of defilements (*kilesa*), volitional activity (*kamma*) and kamma resultant (*vipāka*). The word cycle is a metaphor for a self-feeding process meaning something that moves on and on, endlessly, like the pinions of a clock. Contrarily, Nibbāna represents the final cessation from these three cycles, which function interdependently.

Though Nibbāna is transcendental, being a state of spiritual transformation, it is verifiable because of the verifiability of the enlightenment factors. Since Nibbāna is a reality, a here and now experience, not an idea, there is nothing nebulous about its realization. This is in contrast with the theistic idea of realization of God, Brahman etc. In other words, the realization of Nibbāna, as enlightenment, can be tested here and now. For instance, when one meditates or develops the mind in order to activate and awaken the hidden potentials and reach the transmundane heights of Nibbānic freedom, one of the basic resultant experiences is mindfulness. Without proper attention or being mindful, one just cannot meditate or achieve even a modicum of concentration.

With progress in meditation, as one develops mindfulness, one also develops insight into the working of the mind itself, which means that one investigates the realities thereof. As investigation progresses, the mind becomes energized and effortful, leading to enthusiasm, joy and rapture, in that order. Rapture induces tranquillity. A calm and composed state automatically integrates the mind and unifies its various faculties. This meditative concentration, also known as *samādhi* or absorption, flowers into equanimity, that perfect spiritual equlibrium symbolic of the excellence of enlightenment. With the development of the enlightenment-factors, the aspirant gets rid of the cankers, and is then called "One who has cut off craving, severed the fetters, and, by totally vanquishing pride, has made an end of suffering, indeed!"

This brings us to the core-element of the methodology,

namely, wisdom in action. The centrality of practical wisdom is emphasised in each and every one of the aforesaid seven methods to overcome cankers. The *Sabbāsava Sutta*, invariably repeats that 'wisely reflecting' the aspirant 'lives self-restrained, makes judicious use of basic needs, endures unpleasant and painful experiences, avoids danger, including unbecoming resorts and evil associations, eliminates wrong thoughts etc. and develops the enlightenment-factors.'

Thus, these methods are founded upon wise consideration. Since wise consideration means contemplation of the three characteristics of *anicca*, *dukkha* and *anatta*, and of the Four Noble Truths, the whole procedure ultimately boils down to wisdom in action, which the Buddha, calls sagacity, *nepakka* (from *nipaka*) (See *Karnaṇīya Metta Sutta, Sutta Nipāta*).

It has been mentioned that the last method, consisting of the development of the seven enlightenment-factors, is the most vital of them all. It is so because cultivating the enlightenment-factors in effect is wisdom in action in the most operative sense of the term. And sagacity here stands for all thirty seven *Bodhipakkiyā* Dhammas, which are called the 'requisites for enlightenment.'

This brings us to the verse in which the Buddha refers to sagacity as wisdom in action, as the focal point of the Noble Eightfold Path, and as the confluence where the inborn and the acquired spiritual qualities co-mingle to bring about spiritual perfection.

Here is an interesting episode mentioned in the *Saṃyutta Nikāya.* A certain *deva* (deity) approached the Buddha in the night and, to clear himself of certain doubts, asked this question:

*"There is tangle within, there is tangle without,*
*Beings are fully enmeshed in the tangle:*
*I therefore ask you, Gotama, please,*
*Who can disentangle this tangle?"* (S.I.55).

The Buddha replied:

*"Having established oneself well in virtue,*
*When a wise man develops*
*The higher consciousness and insight,*
*Then, being ever-ardent and sagacious,*
*This monk alone disentangles the tangles."* (*S*.I.56)
*"Those whose passion, hatred and ignorance*
*Have altogether been expurgated,*
*These canker-freed, are accomplished ones;*
*They alone disentangle the tangle.* (*S*.I.57)
*"Where both mind and matter,*
*Without remainder have ceased,*
*So too sensory-reactions and perception of form,*
*There all tangles are rent asunder."* (*S*.I.58)

From the standpoints of both practical psychology and realistic philosophy, these three verses have profound implications. The first verse adumbrates the path of spiritual purification. The second focuses upon the realization of the highest supramundane state of the Arahat, the *asekha*, one who is no longer striving but has become a Master himself. The third one uncovers the objective reality of Nibbāna as the transcendent, the absolute dimension of freedom, contact with which transforms the mind into the supramundane element (*Nibbāna-dhātu*).

The first verse consists of six fertile themes which together cover the entire range of spiritual practice or the path to perfection. These are: 'wise man', 'virtue', 'higher consciousness', 'insight', 'ardent' and 'sagacious'.

Here 'virtue' means *sīla*, purification of morality. Higher consciousness implies the eight *samāpattis* or supernormal attainments, based on absorptions, *samādhi*. The word 'ardent' refers to a degree of zeal and vigour which is capable of burning off the defilements. The remaining three terms have specific connotations, though all, signify the faculty of wisdom.

'Wise man, established in virtue' etc., refers to one possessing innate or native wisdom, that is, an endowment at birth as a result of past wholesome *kammas*. It is only a person with an inborn wisdom, in the form of a capacity to see through and discriminate instinctively, without logical or step-by-step thinking, who can understand the value of moral and spiritual endeavour, who can separate the good from the bad and always choose the positive approach.

Technically, such a man is known as *tihetuka puggala*—a person whose rebirth-consciousness stands firmly established in the three wholesome roots (*hetu*) of non-greed, non-hatred and non-delusion. Though expressed in negative forms, these terms express exceedingly positive mental conditions or functions. Non-greed, for instance, means generosity, charity, large-heartedness and similar positive qualities. Non-hatred refers to love, compassion, goodwill, sympathy and the like. Similarly, non-delusion implies wisdom, knowledge, insight, understanding etc. Thus, a being who is reborn with a powerful mental equipment capable of penetrating into the actualities of things, must necessarily be so conditioned and oriented to innately opt for the path of morality, mental development and insight.

"Insight", the second of the three aspects, refers to the development of *vipassanā* or insight-meditation, and therewith the supramundane path and fruition insights.

The term 'sagacious' means practical wisdom, that is to say, the ability to apply the higher supramudane insights in the day-to-day transactions of life. Here the wisdom faculty is translated into an expert skill to carry out the mundane responsibilities and to carve out a way of life that, while maintaining its contact with the transcendent or higher insights, yet plants itself squarely on the practical requirements. And all this without any compromise, either with the spirit or with the letter of the Dhamma, the Truth.

The sagacious man, combining as he does the aforesaid three specific aspects of wisdom with virtue, meditative absorptions and ardent spiritual quest, thus, is the very epitome of spiritual perfection. And it is he who has the necessary mastery and power with which to cut asunder the tangle of the *āsavas*. Practical wisdom, expressing inner maturity and discernment, therefore is at the core of the seven methods to overcome the cankers.

Practical wisdom is synonymous with wise consideration, the heart of spiritual life and the foundation on which the mansion of deliverance (*vimokkha*) is built. If not for wise thinking, life would be despoiled by the cankers (*āsavas*).

To consider wisely is to weigh things well in one's mind, to deliberate the reasons for and against, to reflect and reason out as opposed to being impulsive, and to intentionally determine the right course, having analysed and separated the right from the wrong and the good from the bad.

This wholesome mental activity of weighing things up is what determines the course of one's life—whether life is to be progressive or retrogressive, whether one's conduct is to be purposive and beneficial or to get more to the contrary, whether one is more involved in *kamma* and fettered helplessly to recurring existence, or one is to wrench oneself from the grip of *kamma* and find access unto the supramundane dimension of spiritual liberation—*Nibbāna*. There is no sitting on the fence; there is nothing in between good and evil, nothing in between wise and unwise consideration.

When the mind is in the grip of *āsavas*, all thoughts, urges and other mental activities become distorted. If the mind is deconditioned and set right, and one learns to view life in a new perspective against the backdrop of reality, that is, in terms of the three characteristics *anicca*, *dukkha, anatta*, then life becomes a spiritual adventure into deliverance.

The pilgrimage from the dark states of *āsavas* to the states of light of the *vimokkhas*, is indeed a great challenge and an accomplishment. But the task, so arduous and vital, is entirely dependent upon how one thinks, considers, and weighs up the pros and cons, every moment, and at every step of one's advancement.

# Chapter 13

## Mental 'Contraband'

The word 'contraband' conjures up the mental picture of something that is counter to law and order, sometimes to the economy of the land. In practical terms, it stands for smuggled articles and for an illegal black market transactions. Contraband things feed the greed and acquisitiveness of a few, to the detriment of the law-abiding people. It corrupts the established system meant for catering to people's well-being.

On this analogy, there is a contraband phenomenon in the world of the mind, in the sense of a certain mental activity which runs counter to those psychological laws that maintain the good health and sound performance of the mind. The Buddha identified this psychological contraband and termed it *amanasikaraṇīya*—a thing which should not be considered or inwardly attended to. This is the negatory gerundive form of the term *manasikāra*, which means to 'attending to' or 'looking at' which means to consider, deliberate or regard.

Why is a certain 'consideration' or 'attention' deemed mental contraband? Is it because it contravenes a given convention or law, or controverts an ideology or a religious system? No. But since it injures and infects the mind itself with which it arises together and co-exists, it is deemed mental contraband, something to be disallowed and prevented from defiling the mind. Just as rust, arising from iron, eats into it, even so, a wrong consideration, arising from the mind, ruins it, eats into it, pollutes and corrupts it, impedes its progress and edification, debilitates it and destroys all its higher potentials. Wrong consideration creates mental ulcers from which *āsavas* ooze out, to corrupt the mind, leading to moral and spiritual deterioration.

Defining the wrongness of a consideration, the Buddha has said: "It is a wrong consideration because, on one hand, the 'unarisen canker arises', and, on the other, 'an arisen canker increases'—*anuppannā ceva āsavā uppajjanti, uppannā ca āsavā pavaḍḍhanti.* The criterion, here, is objective and factual, not doctrinal.

Whatever consideration brings about the arising of sensuality (*kāmāsava*), the egocentric survival-drive (*bhavāsava*), the ideological obscurantism and dogmatism (*diṭṭhāsaṿa*) and mental blindness and ignorance (*avijjāsava*), it is, by its very nature, wrong and unwise, in the same way as fire, by its very nature, burns, consumes and destroys. Just as industrial effluents pollute the environment—land, water, air and endanger life, so do the mental effluents—*āsavas*. An *āsava* defiles the mind by its polluting (*kilesa*), corroding (*saṅkilesa*), and corrupting (*upakkilesa*) influence; it weakens the mind, keeps it under the thraldom of *kamma* and rebirth, and thereby binds a being onto the wheel of becoming (*saṃsāra-bandhana*) and impedes his spiritual progress.

Accordingly, an *āsava* has been described as (i) the 'fetter' (*saṃyojana*) that keeps one incarcerated in the prison-house of phenomenal existence; (ii) the 'flood' (*ogha*) that inundates and engulfs the mind under the swirling and overpowering currents of craving for sensual pleasure, survival and destructivity, (iii) the mental impediment (*nīvaraṇa*) that creates sensual desires, ill-will, lethargy, restlessness, remorse, doubt and cynicism. These are the psychological implications underlying an unwholesome consideration, hence its contraband nature. In other words, a consideration that, by going against the laws of truth and perfection, beauty and purity smuggles *āsava* into the mind, is basically unwholesome and therefore spiritually unallowable and contraband.

Having explained the nature of *amanasikaraṇīya* or mental contraband and what havoc is wrought by it, it may be asked why and how wrong consideration does arise.

Wrong consideration arises primarily because of a certain belief, view or conviction and when the belief grows into a faith and an ideological commitment, then it becomes a 'free port', a prosperous centre for mental contraband to thrive. The notion of 'I', or ego, or self, is at the root of all wrong considerations. The egocentric drive automatically beclouds the mind and prevents it from comprehending the truth in the same way as the cloud prevents sunshine from reaching the earth. And whoso does not penetrate into the reality of things, can neither understand the mental contraband nor the *āsavas*. That is why the Buddha unequivocally said: "Only for him who understands, who comprehends, is there the destruction of cankers, so I say, not for him who does not understand, who does not comprehend."

Believing that there is an entity called 'I,' self, or soul, a person not only gets involved in philosophical speculation, but also entangles himself in the net of time. He believes that time is real and absolute in nature, while the truth is to the contrary. Time indicates motion, and exists as a concept, idea or conventional measurement of events and happenings; at best it is a relative dimension, with relative functions. Thinking speculatively, man grasps time as the very equation of reality and identifies himself—that is to say, his ego or self or soul—to be the very essence of this reality. Even though everything in the world may change, yet, somehow, this self or soul does not, so he argues. He is even convinced that this time-born 'I' is eternal and immortal.

A belief or a conviction that is essentially false, must pay the price for distorting the truth, and the price is doubt, scepticism or a cynical syndrome. So, he begins to doubt, "Was I in the past or was I not? What was I, how was I? What having been, what then was I? "Similarly, he gets caught in the vicious circle of speculating about the future and the present. He misses the truth that the so-called past, future and present are the illusions created by the flux, the tremendous dynamism, of the consciousness itself. At best, they are concepts, mental constructs, and do not have an absolute quality or substance of their own.

Not having discerned the actuality of time, nor of the egocentric flux, he now is encapsullated within very specific faith patterns, otherwise called religions. Any one of these six perverse views (*diṭṭhi*) arises in him, "There is self in me, or there is no self in me." Thus 'in me' becomes the mental fixation or the fixed metaphysical idea. Or, the view that, "By myself alone do I know of the self or of the non-self'". Here 'myself' is the fixed metaphysical entity. Or, "By my non-self alone do I know of the self". Here, hc conjures up the ridiculous idea of a durable non-self. Or again, the perverse view occurs to him, "Whatever this self is in me that speaks, feels experiences, and that is the result of my past *kamma*, this self is permanent and it lasts as eternity itself." Here, the assumption of a 'self' in the context of changefulness as a fixed soul-entity, speaks of *sassata-diṭṭhi*—eternity-belief. All these beliefs or views appear to him as being 'true and real' because of the self-illusion under which the mind is made to labour.

Self-illusion coexists with superstitions, which are expressed in the form of rites, customs, ritualistic practices, faith in omens, numbers, sights etc. Self-illusion and superstition are accompanied by fear and doubt. The Buddha has called these perverse views to be the womb of self-illusion, of doubt and belief in superstitious practices. They are analogous to the hold of a vice in which one is caught, to a thicket or wilderness, where one gets lost; to a state of tremendous struggle, as is seen in a person who is writhing and wriggling in a fetter. Also, fettered by perverse views, a spiritually unoriented ordinary person is not freed from the wheel of becoming, from birth, from ageing, from death, from sorrowing, lamenting, pain, depression and despair. Emphasised the Buddha, "Indeed, he is not freed from suffering, so I declare."

Having dilated on the what and why of wrong consideration, that is to say, the definition and origin of wrong consideration, it would be interesting to examine how wrong consideration arises, and the mechanism involved in its occurrence. Here again, the *Sabbāsava Sutta* is clear in its enunciation. The instrument that creates wrong consideration is the state of an unheedful, spiritually unmotivated worlding who does not care about wise association and who has no interest in the study and practice of the Dhamma. In other words, bad or worldly company, and lack of spiritual guidance and commitment, constitute the mechanism for the occurrence and prevalence of wrong consideration. So, the answer to the question, "When does wrong consideration arise?", is when one is uninstructed and uninitiated into the teachings of the holy ones, is unheedful of and unconversant with the Teachings of the noble ones, like the Buddhas and the Arahants.

# Chapter 14

## THE INITIATE AND HOLY COMPANY

The spiritual man is characterised by his inspiring conduct, wisdom and pursuit of truth. These traits are in sharp contrast to the ways of the worldly man.

As mentioned in the *Sabbāsava Sutta*, the worldly man "does not understand things which should be considered and which should not be considered." By not rightly understanding he does not rightly consider things and by not considering things rightly, "his unarisen cankers arise and the arisen cankers increase." In other words, he gets thoroughly entangled in the tanglements of the cankers. The wise man, in contradistinction, "understands things which should be considered and which should not be considered." By rightly understanding, he considers rightly, i.e., wisely, and by considering wisely, "his unarisen cankers do not arise and the arisen cankers are overcome."

The wise man is like a skilled forester who enters into a bamboo-thicket unhurt and safe. He proceeds by lopping off the thorny and sharp bamboo-tanglements and returns with the best of bamboo poles. The unwise worldling enters into the bamboo-thicket only to get entangled, thoroughly hurt, even lost or doomed to death, much less returning safely with bamboos.

The pursuit of truth itself constitutes the well-spring whence wise consideration and right understanding flow. That is why the Buddha points out which way the well-instructed noble one's minds are oriented; that is, the minds of noble ones ever are heedful of the Enlightened One and his enlightened disciples (saints), they, assiduously cultivate the company of the holy ones, and thus become adept in their Teachings. "'This is suffering,' so the noble one wisely considers: 'this is the cause of suffering,' so he wisely considers, 'this is the cessation of suffering', so he wisely considers: 'this is the path leading to the cessation of suffering,' so he wisely considers. While thus wisely considering, his three fetters are overcome, *viz.*, self-illusion, doubt and clinging to rules and rituals."

The definition of wise consideration therefore boils down to considering things in terms of the Four Noble Truths, which is the quintessence of the Buddha's discovery and the foundation of his omniscience.

As soon as one looks at things from the viewpoint of the Noble Truths, which the vista unfolding is so edifying that the mind perforce remains beyond the range of the polluting cankers. In the rarified heights of wise consideration, the polluting worldliness and the *āsavas* are overcome and the mind effortlessly remains in a condition of composure, purity and clarity. In such a state, there is no longer the propensity for egocentric thinking or self-centred speech or act. There is no doubt, no fear, and no clinging to superstitions and rituals.

The noble one who 'lives' the Noble Truths, is incapable of transgressing the principles of compassion and love, truthfulness and purity. Such a one cannot be envious or miserly. It is said that he is so firmly rooted in the five precepts, *pañca-sīla*, that his intrinsic power of virtue frees him from all threats of insecurity, strife and unhappiness, to which ordinary persons are prone. He has no need to struggle for survival, nor to toil for a competitive existence. He indeed enjoys peace and happiness because of his commitment to the Noble Truths. He is the 'initiate', whose holy company is ever enlivening and elevating.

Just as getting out of a polluted environment and entering into a fresh and exhilarating atmosphere coincide and happen simultaneously, even so, there is an inevitable concurrence between the abandoning (*pahāna*) of the cankers and the experiencing of the Noble Truths. As already mentioned, the Four Noble Truths constitute a single experience. They are not doctrines. They are experienced together in the same way the four facets of a single gem are simultaniously viewed.

The Four Noble Truths form the essence or the realities, of things. They signify the actualization of the truths of life, of the world, of the Beyond, and of the path leading thereto. This is reflected in the transformation of the mind from the limited, ego-bound existence to the boundlessness of Nibbāna.

# Chapter 15

## OVERCOMING CANKERS

The goal of Buddha-Dhamma is Nibbāna, which is a specific realization, and an unambiguous accomplishment.

Nibbāna has been described by various metaphors, such as: *paramaṃ sukhaṃ*—the most blissful; *dukkhassa nirodho*—the cessation of suffering; *saṃsāra-vaṭṭatọ vimocanaṃ*—liberation from the vicious circle of worldly existence; *kamma-punabbhava-bandanato mutti*—emancipation from the bondage of *kamma* and rebirth; *anāsavo*—the canker-free state; *asaṃkhataṃ*—the unconditioned*; amataṃ*—the immortal; *paṇītaṃ*—the exalted; *santaṃ*—the peaceful; *dhuvaṃ*—the eternal; *lokuttaraṃ*—the supramundane or transcendental; *vimokkhaṃ*—the state of deliverance; *akataṃ*— the uncreated; *sayambhu*—the self-sustaining; *nissaraṇaṃ*–the ultimate escape, leaving behind; *khemaṃ*– final security; *saranaṃ*—the refuge; and a number of other very meaningful expressions.

*Nissaraṇa-pahāna*—the escape through 'leaving behind' or overcoming is also one of the synonyms of Nibbāna. Here, by 'overcoming' is meant the abandonment of worldly existence, through transcendental insight, thus finding access unto the final liberation. The escape, the deathless, here means escape into the Supreme Good, (*summum bonum*), eternal and blissful state of the Absolute, where all struggles and sufferings intrinsic in phenomenal existence have ceased totally ended. Nibbāna, thus, has been construed as an overcoming in its supramundane aspect. It is like when a child becomes a young man. The state of youth signifies an outgrowing or abandoning of the state of childhood.

In the day-to-day transactions of mundane life, the word overcoming is often used in the sense of removing by way of substitution or replacement. That is, removing something by bringing in another thing. Here the principle of substitution by a positive alternative, *e.g.* substituting or replacing anger by love is meant. In this *sutta* five of the seven methods, that is, except the first and the seventh, use this term 'overcoming' in the sense of substitution by a positive alternative. For instance, substituting the mind-defiling negative factors by positive alternatives or opposite virtues. When hate is ruining one's life by expressing itself in the form of acts of killing, one undertakes the moral precept of non-destruction of life. (*pāṇātipātā veramaṇī sikkhāpadaṃ*). Thus, by the substitution of inoffensiveness and non-violence, one abandons violence and hate.

To use a modern anology, it is like regenerating a stagnant economy, where there is the policy of 'import-substitution' to conserve foreign exchange and enhance the country's finances and thereby stop avoidable drainage in other areas. In the same way, by substituting a negative, unwholesome factor with a positive, wholesome one, a seeker of truth conserves spiritual energy, enhances moral power and stops the wastage of precious talent and potential.

To use another analogy, just as, by making available an effective alternative, a substitution-product not only enables the scientific and technological progress to be maintained, but it also actually brings about a further growth in the search for better performance and function. Even so, a spiritual substitute for a mundane function, always brings about an enhancement of progress in any field.

A sympathetic doctor will use his skills better than a cold, unsympathetic doctor, however capable he may be. A humane engineer will raise production invariably by bringing about good, interpersonal relationships between labour and management. An honest public servant will bring greater welfare and justice in society than a corrupt one, however suave and efficient the latter may be. A helpful policeman is even more effective a protector of the masses than an oppressive one. A contented tradesman creates a balanced economy, enabling everyone to be above want. A humble and service-minded politician serves the country and the people far more purposefully and efficiently than a bumptious and crafty one, however successful he may be in holding on to power.

From a transcendental cessation to a pragmatic substitution is a vast gamut, which the principle of overcoming covers.

Overcoming of cankers constitutes a tremendous, mind-liberating act—*cetovimutti.* In this sense it is the equivalent of *vimokkha* a state of deliverance which occurs at various levels. The *Visuddhi-magga* mentions three levels at which the overcoming of cankers takes place. These are at the levels of:

*Sīla*—Moral purification, through a life of virtue.

*Samādhi*—Purification of mind, through meditative absorptions.

*Paññā*—Purification of wisdom, through insight-meditations.

Morality enables one to overcome cankers and defilements by way of substitution—*tadaṅga pahāna.* Virtue substitutes an evil act by a positive, good act.

Meditative absorptions enable one to overcome cankers by way of subduing the five mental hindrances, which method is called *vikkhambhana pahāna.* By bringing the mind to a state of perfect concentration and composure, meditative absorptions (*jhāna*) enable one to remove or suspend those mental hindrances or obstacles which keep the mind in a state of disquiet and fragmentation. By cultivating the *samatha*-meditations, as one brings about a unification of mental powers and faculties, the mind is enabled to rise to a higher level, beyond the sensory, into those sublime states of consciousness known as absorption—*samādhi*. Various supernormal attainments and psychic powers are achieved through these sublime states of consciousness.

Wisdom enables one to overcome cankers and defilements by way of uprooting these fetters—*upaccheda pahāna*. By cultivating the insight-meditations (*vipassanā*), as one develops the intuitive insights of the supramundane paths and fruitions *(magga-phala-ñāṇa*), one accomplishes a transformation of the mind by uprooting the fetters, that is to say, the cankers and defilements (*āsavas* and *kilesas*).

At the mundane level of *tadaṅga pahāna*, *i.e.* substituting evil by virtue, the mind achieves the heightened purification that morality brings about. Through this stage of moral purification, one can be assured of a better, prosperous and peaceful living, here and now, as well as a happy destiny (*sugati*) hereafter *i.e.* a happy rebirth in the human and divine planes of existence.

At the sublime state of the *vikkhambhana-pahāna*, *i.e.*, subduing mental hindrances and gaining the meditative absorptions, the mind achieves that divine level of rarified purification which the *samādhis* bring about. Through this stage of sublimated mental purification, one can be assured of a totally unified, suprasensory and paranormal state of consciousness forming the base of psychic or supernatural powers. It is a very blissful attainment (*diṭṭhadhamma-sukhavihāra*), to be enjoyed here and now and in a sublime rebirth among the high divinities of the *rūpa* and *arūpāvacara* brahmas (the subtle-form and formless spheres).

At the transcendental level of *samuccheda-pahāna, i.e.*, uprooting of the fetters leading to the transformation of consciousness from the mundane to the supramundane, the mind attains to that matchless purification which the intuitive insights accomplish.[1] Through this stage of supramundane purification, one can be assured of that state of spiritual excellence which is born of transformation, wrought by the realization of *Nibbāna*—the unconditioned Absolute. As the object of the supramundane path and fruition-insight states of consciousness, Nibbāna brings about a total and irreversible change of the personality, whereby he or she is no more subject to rebirth in any states of woe (*duggati*). It is that exalted condition that marks the attainment of escape from all bondages of a limited, defiled mind, from *kammas* and their corollary rebirths, in lower planes of existence, and from the unmitigated suffering which the struggle for existence entails.

Apart from these threefold modes of overcoming the cankers, the sacred Pāli scriptures also mention two other modes, namely, (a) overcoming defilements by way of tranquillisation - *paṭippassaddhi-pahāna*, which comes about through the achievement of *phala-samāpatti,* the supramundane fruition absorptions, and (b) overcoming defilements by way of escape *nissaraṇa-pahāna*, consequent upon the realization of Nibbāna. The absolute 'escape' here, implies a variety of shades of meaning such as, outgrowing and transcending *saṃsāra*, reaching the further end and thus 'avoiding, averting and surmounting' the existential sufferings. That is to say, by 'escaping' one wrests immunity from the maladies and deliverance from the bondage of *kamma* and rebirth.

As the enlightened disciples of the Buddha known as noble ones *(ariya)* attain the various transcendental path-insights, *i.e.* of *sotāpatti* (stream-entrance), *sakadāgāmi* (once-returning), *anāgāmi* (non-returning), and *arahatta* (perfection), the tenfold fetters which keep a being tied to the wheel of becoming (*bhava-cakka*), are progressively uprooted, commensurate with a particular path. With the annihilation of the fetters, an ineffable stillness sets in as the subsequent fruition-moments of a given path arise; this supramundane stillness constitutes the

1. Impurities are 'banes' and 'taints' because they destroy things, according to the *Dhammapada*.

overcoming by tranquillization. The overcoming by escape is a synonym of the overcoming co-existent with cessation (Nibbāna), as mentined above. These two modes, therefore, belong to the transcendental level accomplished by *samuccheda-pahāna*—overcoming by uprooting.

The Pāli canon also provides telling analogies to elucidate the fivefold modes of overcoming cankers.

Just as the darkness of the night is dispelled by the lighting of a lamp, even so, by *tadaṅga pahāna* (substituting evil by good), one does away with all unwholesome mental states and wrong conduct that impede moral and spiritual advancement. One's inner edification and happiness are thereby ensured.

Just as the impact of the bang of a vessel on an algae-ridden pond pushes the algae away, even so by *vikkhambhana-pahāna* (subduing mental hindrances), one keeps down all negative and adverse factors and enables the mind to be transported into the sublime heights of the absorptions.

Just as a tree destroyed by lightning can never grow again, even so, by *samuccheda-pahāna* (uprooting fetters through path and fruition-insights), the defilements and cankers are for ever destroyed, can never sprout again, thus enabling one to be established in the irreversible dimension of the transcendent, whence there is no more a fall-back into the mundane.

Just as the stillness following a storm creates a profound tranquillity, even so does *paṭippassadhi-pahāna* (the tranquillization by the supramundane fruition-absorptions), enables one to enjoy the bliss of the ineffable spiritual peace that follows the breakthrough occasioned by the supramundane path-insights.

Just as inexplicable security and assurance follows an escape from a great peril or calamity, even so does *nissaraṇa-pahāna* (the escape reflective of emancipation from *saṃsāra*), bestows that supreme security which coexists with 'cessation', the utterly bond-free, deathless state of Nibbāna.

The Omniscient Buddha, in his all-embracing compassion

for beings seeking freedom from the bondage of *kamma* and recurring existence, enunciated the seven-fold technique of overcoming cankers in the *Sabbāsava Sutta*. Said the Buddha, "There are cankers to be overcome by insight, there are cankers to be overcome by self control, there are cankers to be overcome by judicious use, there are cankers to be overcome by endurance, there are cankers to be overcome by avoidance, there are cankers to be overcome by elimination, there are cankers to be overcome by development."

The simple is truly beautiful and profound. So is this simple and practical instruction of the Omniscient Buddha. These seven methods comprise every conceivable situation in life, and at all levels. Under whatever circumstances a seeker of truth may be placed, he or she is bound to find the appropriate weapon in this fully-equipped armoury of the seven methods to fight cankers, in whatever intensity or masquerade they may arise. These seven methods are the practical applications that translate the five modes (*tadaṅga* etc.) of overcoming cankers which have been already discussed with appropriate analogies.

Here, by 'overcoming through insight', is to be understood, in particular, *samuccheda pahāna*—overcoming by uprooting the fetters. The *Sabbāsava Sutta* mentions only the first three fetters, namely, self-illusion (*sakkāya-diṭṭhi*), sceptical doubt (*vicikicchā*) and superstitious adherance to rules and rituals (*sīlabbata-parāmāsa*), which are annihilated by the supra-mundane insight of the stream-entrance. However, as a technique, the implication of 'overcoming by insight' could also mean the overcoming of the remaining seven fetters through the three remaining Path-insights.

As insight is an indispensable factor at every level of the process of overcoming, substitution and subduing effects should also be easy to obtain through it, in the same way as a long-distance swimmer can easily cover short distances. The Paṭisambhidā-magga mentions a number of methods of overcoming, amounting to substitution and subduing by the application of insight. For instance, it is said that through the application of insight as a virtue of restraint (*ñāṇa-saṃvara*), one overcomes the propensity for killing, stealing, sexual misconduct or lying, back-biting, abusing and gossiping, or covetousness, ill-will and wrong views. Similarly, by the application of insight, one can rouse the urge for renunciation and overcome the proneness to lust and acquisitiveness; or through good-will, love and compassion, one can overcome hatred, resentment and cruelty; or by rousing the perception of light and a sense of urgency for action, one can overcome mental inertia and laziness; or through mindfulness and meditative concentration, one can overcome distraction and mental fragmentation; or by appropriate knowledge one can overcome doubt. These are methods of substitution and subduing fashioned by the deft hands of insight.

The *Sutta* is forthright and wholly unambiguous in spelling out the contents of insight in the form of the Four Noble Truths, "This is suffering, this is the cause of suffering, this is the cessation of suffering, this is the path leading to the cessation of suffering, so he wisely considers"—points out the Supremely Enlightened Buddha.

As one discerns the fact of impermanence and changefulness intrinsic in life—in every desire or urge, in every fond hope or aspiration, in every action and toil—one is bound to see through this state of *saṃsāric* instability as a condition of involvement and unsatisfactoriness. For, the ego that craves for and strives to find, longs to hold on to, and to supersede, represents that illusion which directly subverts this truth of *saṃsāric* instability. It makes use of numberless masquerades and ruses, alas, only to aggravate the entanglement and the anguish and misery that go with it. Struggle is possible and toil is inevitable, only where instability is basic. Therefore, when one identifies these inherent factors of instability and unsatisfactoriness as characterising life in depth, one is not far away from the actuality also of the unsubstantial nature of life.

When life is conditioned by ever so many factors, in ever so many ways, and surely in a changing context, where is the place then for a non-changing entity? If there were, one would be immortal and ever-liberated, which one obviously is not, which is to say that life is essentially an impersonal process, dependent on conditions—*paccayā*.

This identification of the triple characteristics of instability, involvement and unsubstantiality is the essence of the insight into the truth of suffering, which means, in a wider sense, not only misery and pain, but the all-pervasive imperfection and unsatisfactoriness that characterize everything that is, every form of existence, every mundane dimension!

The penetration into the truth of suffering also upholds the knowledge of its origin, *i.e.* craving, with all its multi-dimensional ramifications—the sensual syndrome, the survival-obsession, and the suicidal psychosis. The twin insight facets of the gem, in perspective, naturally bring into view the contrasting outlines of the transcendental where both suffering and its cause do not obtain, as well as the path leading to this matchless dimension.

This fourfold simultaneous vision is the meditative experience that insight-meditations give rise to, leading to self-transformation. Hence the Buddha's perspicuous definition of insight as being a clear comprehension of the Four Noble Truths, intrinsic in a 'wise consideration'. Notwithstanding meditative experience, even as a purely intellectual exercise, if a sincere seeker were to train and familiarise his mind, a time would certainly come when this fourfold insight would be clearly grasped and conceptualized, and to that extent his mind is de-conditioned of the delusions that mistake the non-essential to be essential, and the unreal to be real, and imagine life to be stable, blissful and self-based! This is no mean achievement in a world so frankly contrary and perverse because of the absence of this insight.

A learned man who does not keep brushing up his knowledge, loses what he knows. Non-repetition thus is the bane of a learned man; it is the impurity that mars his learning. A doctor who does not refresh his mind with the latest developments can be not only out-of-date, but positively dangerous to the patient because of the stagnation that he has brought about in his knowledge and skill. Stagnation is a bane, a ruin caused by decay and whatever decays becomes an impurity.

Just as rust sprung from iron eats it away, even so, the impurities of mind eat into it, pollute and weaken it. Even the poshest of mansions, when neglected and kept unkempt, become dilapidated; a most beautiful girl, if she is slothful, loses her charm; a sentry who is not watchful will bring the enemy's wrath upon the entire force.

These are some of the examples found in the *Dhammapada* that highlight the need for constant application to keep the mind free from the impurities resulting from cankers. These applications differ according to the need of the occasion. That is why the *Sabbāsava Sutta* provides seven very distinct methods of application, which are to be used appropriately befitting the situation.

The first of these seven methods is the method whereby one overcomes cankers by the application of insight. Although already discussed in detail, this immensely vital topic permits repetition. Insight is specifically underlined because it is the one supreme weapon that can effectively and fully eradicate the worst and the most tenacious of all impurities, the canker of ignorance.

Again, the *Dhammapada* emphasises, "Unchastity is the taint in woman: niggardliness is the taint in a giver: whether here or hereafter, all evil things are taints: but a worse taint than these is ignorance. Indeed, it is the worst of all taints."

And ignorance is not just absence of knowledge, but also the perversion of it. It means a false and distorted understanding of truth, in particular, the Four Noble Truths.

The remaining are the methods of self-control, judicious use, endurance, avoidance, elimination and of development. The cankers arise through the senses; therefore they are to be overcome through the instrumentality of control over the senses. If one does not apply control over the senses, they will surely go haywire. One need not mentally attend to whatever sight falls on the avenue of the eye. For instance, to be too curious about the opposite sex or about objects that involve the mind in an unwholesome way, is not being prudent. If one can exert self-restraint over the proclivity towards attractive things, one certainly would enjoy well-being and peace here and now. This is how one does not give the cankers an opportunity to meddle with one's mind, and thereby safeguards one's happiness.

Again, there are cankers that arise when certain basic day-to-day needs such as, food, clothing, shelter etc. are misused or wrongly and ineffectively utilized. If one eats to satisfy one's gluttony, or to show off and pamper one's vanity, or to become fat or thin and delude oneself and others, certainly the basic requisite of eating then becomes a cause for self-destruction rather than self-sustenance. The technique for overcoming the cankers that arise through these basic needs is a wise reflection about the purpose and function of these needs for living meaningfully. For instance, if one uses clothes wisely as one should, for warding off inclemencies of weather and keeping oneself healthy and decent, and if one does not allow oneself to be conditioned by external factors like fashion etc., then the act of clothing oneself will become an aid for becoming mature in life.

There are cankers that grow within only because one does not know how and when to forbear and forgive. The Buddha has said that the greatest penance is enduring patience. If only one can be patient at the appropriate moment, a great deal of embarrassment, disputation and unpleasantness could be averted and life could be made indeed pleasant and worth living. A timely break in the impetuous reaction to somebody's remarks, or the sagacious acceptance of some of the painful and unfortunate life-situations—adversities, diseases and disappointments, would nip in the bud of cankers that otherwise would become burdensome and consuming.

There are cankers that will overtake the mind unless appropriate measures are taken to frustrate them. There is the delightful story in the *Jātaka* of the filthy hog who was defeated by his very abject victory. The uncouth pig challenged the lord of the forest to a duel. The lion, who could have torn him into pieces, pitied his recklessness and thought it more prudent and the better part of valour to give him time to ruminate over the consequences of such an absurdly rash proposition. Accepting the lion's suggestion, the pig wallowed in a cesspool for days and then went to the lion as a challenger on equal terms! The lion rightly avoided the filthy boar, thus conceding him his ludicrous victory. There are many situations and things which should be wisely avoided. A foolhardy attitude of meeting them only allows the cankers to defile the mind. For instance, an unbecoming resort, improper association or bad company can mar one's life totally. Sagacious avoidance, therefore, is eloquent testimony to one's sense of proportion and right approach.

There are cankers that arise solely through wrong thinking. Therefore, if one eliminates wrong thoughts, the cankers too are eliminated. If one orients one's thinking in the right direction, the elimination of wrong thoughts such as sensuality, ill-will or cruelty, in whatever guise they may arise, will be automatically achieved. Here, constant mindfulness is the most important element for the success of this technique.

The last method, known as overcoming cankers through development, calls for the cultivation of certain positive spiritual qualities, (the enlightenment-factors) as distinct from the application of other approaches such as elimination etc. It is relevant to every situation in life, which thereby reflects its supreme efficacy. Apart from ensuring well-being here and now, it also guarantees the security of the transcendental.

These extremely practical modes of self-culture and self-purification, when successfully exercised, bring matchless accomplishments as is eloquently pronounced by the Buddha in these concrete terms, "He has cut off craving, uprooted the fetters, and, by totally vanquishing pride, it is he who has made an end of suffering indeed."

# Chapter 16

## NIBBEDHIKA-PARIYĀYA SUTTA[1]

### (Penetration)[2]

In this discourse the Buddha expounds a system of analysis called 'the method of penetration' for cultivating intuitive insight and to rid the mind of all cankers. A translation of that portion of the *Nibbedhika Sutta,* which deals with the penetration of cankers is presented here.

1."Monks, I shall expound to you this spiritual method called 'the method of penetration of reality'. Listen well and keep it in mind. I shall speak."

"Yes, most venerable Sir", replied those monks to the Blessed One. And the Blessed One spoke thus:

"And, monks what is that spiritual method, which constitutes the method of penetration of reality? Monks, the sense-desires ... the feelings ... the perceptions ... the cankers ... the action ... the suffering should be penetrated; the conditioned origination of suffering should be penetrated; the variety of suffering should be penetrated; the result of suffering should be penetrated; the cessation of suffering should be penetrated; the path leading to the cessation of suffering should be penetrated.

"Monks, the cankers should be penetrated, the conditioned origination of cankers should be penetrated, the variety of cankers should be penetrated, the result of cankers should be

1. *Aṅguttara Nikāya*, III, 410f.
2. Tr. by Acharya Buddharakkhita

penetrated, the cessation of cankers should be penetrated, the path leading to the cessation of cankers should be penetrated. So it has been said. Why was this said?

"Monks, there are these three cankers—the canker of sense-desire, the canker of the desire for becoming and the canker of ignorance.

"Monks, what is the conditioned origination of cankers? Ignorance is the conditioned originaiton of cankers.

"Monks, what is the variety of cankers? There are cankers leading one to hell, there are cankers leading one to the animal state, there are cankers leading one to the plane of ghosts, there are cankers leading one to the human world, there are cankers leading one to the realms of gods. Monks, this is called the variety of cankers.

"Monks, what is the result of cankers? That which when subjected to ignorance, materializes according to that condition of ignorance, this or that individualised existence, either in a meritorious or a demeritorious plane of existence; Monks, this is called the result of cankers.

"Monks, what is the cessation of cankers? The cessation of ignorance is the cessation of cankers. And this very Noble Eightfold Path is the way leading to the cessation of cankers, namely, right understanding, right thought, right speech, right action, right livelihood, right effort, right mindfulness, and right meditative concentration.

"Monks, to the extent, the noble disciple comprehends the cankers in this way, comprehends the conditioned origination of cankers in this way, comprehends the variety of cankers in this way, comprehends the result of cankers in this way, comprehends the cessation of cankers in this way, comprehends the path leading to the cessation of cankers in this way, to that extent he comprehends this holy life to be the way of penetrating the supramundane insight and the cessation of cankers.

"Monks, when it was said, 'The cankers should be

penetrated, the conditioned origination of cankers should be penetrated, the variety of cankers should be penetrated, the result of cankers should be penetrated, the cessation of cankers should be penetrated, the path leading to the cessation of cankers should be penetrated,' it was said with reference to this."

# Chapter 17

## PROBING INTO LIFE

Penetration implies piercing, cleaving, dissecting and penetration of life means to probe into, analyse and discern its complex nature, its intricate working and the underlying laws responsible for all this. It is only when one comprehends the laws which govern life, that one discovers not only its real essence, but also how it is originated, how it is liberated and the path that leads to its liberation.

Life can be compared to a machine. To get the best out of a machine, one should know its mechanism well. The look and cost of the machine would mean very little unless its working is understood. To get the best out of life, one should know its mechanism, *i.e.* the various processes, how it works, how to mend, malfunction, how to enhance its performance to its optimum level etc.

In the *Nibbedhika Sutta*—Discourse on Penetrative Wisdom, the Buddha, in his inimitable way, has clearly explained exactly how this mechanism of life works, how to set right any malfunciton of the various processes and how to optimize life's possibilities. Here, life has been reduced to its bare components, with an analysis of how these work individually and collectively. Then, the basic laws governing this complex life-mechanism have been spelt out so that the truth-seeker is enabled to accomplish his own self-discovery and self-mastery.

There are basic components, in the form of dormant tendencies (*anusaya)* and primordial kammic forces that constitute life's mechanism. These, as presented in this sutta are as follows: *kāma*—sense-desires, *vedanā*—feelings, *saññā*— perceptions, *āsava*—cankers, *kamma*-action, *dukkha*-suffering.

As one is born into the world, equipped with the fivefold senses and the mind, at parturition itself a liaison is established with the external world, as the senses interact with their objects. These purely sensory subject-object interactions—eye with sight, ear with sound, nose with smell, tongue with taste, body with touch, and the mind with mental objects (concepts or ideas) give rise to sense-impression (*phassa*), and therewith many other mental factors co-existing with a state of consciousness.

It is like a railway-train. As soon as the engine moves, a dozen or more bogies also move. Though the engine has its specific function and each bogie its own, nonetheless they are all linked and operating together, to fulfil a common task.

A state of consciousness, according to the teachings of the Buddha, consists of a number of mental factors. All these are born together and function in unison. In doing so, as each one fulfils its specific task, together they contribute to the total function of the given consciousness.

Thus, with the arising of the sense impression there also arise, feeling, perception, volition, and if it is an unwholesome state of consciousness, the canker and many other factors. Since it is an action causing attachment, bondage and involvement, this complex is essentially imperfect and unsatisfactory and is therefore called 'a mass of suffering'—*dukkhak khandha*. This is the mechanics of life in its barest detail, conditionally co-produced and therefore inherently defective and unlike anything that is unconditioned.

It is only the unconditioned that is perfect and wholly desirable, in contradistinction to whatever is conditioned, which is imperfect and undesirable.

*Dukkha*—suffering—in Buddhist parlance, is not merely

pain, misfortune or misery. Even more, it implies an imperfect condition, an unsatisfactory involvement and recurring existence, which is thus a vicious circle. However, when life is transformed through spiritual development, *i.e.,* by a reversal of the worldly process, it indeed becomes blissful.

# Chapter 18

## PERSISTING COMPULSIONS

It would be seen that the sensual urge or desire (*kāma*) is conditionally originated through the influence or inducement of feeling and perception. It is to be emphasised that feeling and perception are the two specific coexistent factors, known as *citta-saṅkhāra*, mental formation, which by experiencing and interpreting respectively the sense-impression, and there-with the sense object, set the canker into operation and thereby an action-pattern, leading to involvement in *dukkha*.

These six factors—sense-desire, feeling, perception, canker, action and suffering work conjointly. And as they do so, they also inter-dependently operate the three cycles (*vaṭṭa*) of defilement, action and result (*kilesa, kamma* and *vipāka*). *Kāma* and *āsava* form a network of complex compulsions representing the dynamics of life. This network stands for the *kilesa-vaṭṭa*- the defilement-cycle. *Kamma* represents the *kamma-vaṭṭa*—the action-cycle and the rest—*vedanā*, *saññā* and *dukkha* —comprise the *vipāka-vaṭṭa*—the resultant-cycle. These six factors of *kāma* etc., working together with the three cycles of *kilesa* etc., representing the *Paṭiccasamuppāda*, the Law of Dependent Origination, has been clearly explained as a precise interdependent operation in the *Nibbedhika-sutta*.

The subjective-objective interaction, implied by the word *kāma*, sets up the *vipāka* cycle—with sense-impression and the two other co-existent accessories of feeling and perception. With the *vipāka*-cycle in motion, the *kilesa*-cycle (*kāma* and *āsava)* too, moves and in turn operates the *kamma*-cycle in that order. As found in the Law of Dependent Origination, the present life starts with *vipāka-vaṭṭa*, *i.e.* rebirth consciousness *(paṭisandhi-viññāṇa)* etc., constituting the passive aspect of the personality. This resultant-cycle gives rise to *taṇhā* and *upādāna*, forming the *kilesa-vaṭṭa*, which in turn sets in motion *bhava* (becoming) or the *kamma*-cycle, constituting the active aspect of life.

The penetration-methodology also analyses how these six factors of *kāma* etc. originate, how they cease and the path which leads to their cessation. Further, the analysis identifies two very interesting aspects. That is to say, the ramifications or variety of each of these factors, as well as the result entailed by these factors in their diverse forms.

The analysis is altogether precise and comprehensive. That is why it is a very effective method of practising *vipassanā*—insight-meditation.

*Kāma* is both subjective and objective. Subjectively, it is sense-desire in a broad way, having a number of facets. Objectively, it is called the strands of the senses—*kāma-guṇa*, that is to say, the fivefold sense-objects of sight, sound, smell, taste and touch, which constitute the stimulants for the senses to respond. They are also called 'pleasures to be enjoyed by the senses', hence the term *kāmanīya* - pleasurable objects.

As the popular connotation of *kāma* is more a psychological state or condition, arising through the agency of the senses, it may be asked how the purely external things constituting the objects of the senses are also termed as *kāma*. In the Pāli canonical work *Niddesa*, it is said, "What is objective kāma? It is the pleasurable sight, sound, smell, taste and touch." From this definition it can be inferred that because these pleasant objects of the senses give rise to a desire to enjoy them, and because this sense-desire, which arises is basically dependent on them, based on them, and on account of them, they also share this common appellation.

The *Nibbedhika Sutta*, however, makes a clear distinction between what it calls the strands of sense-desires, and the sense-desires by themselves. These strands, or the objects of the senses are not, strictly speaking, *kāma* in the sense of that mental condition which colours the mind, defiles it and weakens it. Subjective *kāma* creates a slakeless thirst for pleasure and breeds a canker which, by acting as a mental effluent, pollutes and disturbs the mental ecology thereby hindering spiritual progress. On the contrary, objective *kāma* is not itself an impediment, though it rouses one.

From the synonyms of *kāma* found in the *Abhidhamma*, one can easily make out the all-inclusive import psychologically, ethically and philosophically of this term, as a subjective urge for enjoying the feelings or sensations which arise due to the interactions between the senses and the sense-objects. For instance, when the eye is in healthy condition and a visible object impinges thereon, the sense-impression arising through this interaction brings about a number of other mental factors such as feeling, perception, volition, intention, attention, application, desire or craving etc. All these mental factors arise together and co-exist and are mutually associated and function interdependently; they also pass away together, since they have the same object and the same sense-base at the time they arise. Thus they are *ekuppāda ekanirodhā* and *ekālambana-vatthuka*—"they arise together with a state of consciousness as co-nascent factors, they cease together, and they have one and the same sense-object and sense-base."

The synonyms of *kāma* are as follows:

*Kāma* as *taṇhā*—craving: That is, sense-desire as a thirst for enjoyment, for possession and for egocentric gratification. Because this thirst is insatiable, craving has been compared to a stream or river which flows on and on.

*Kāma* as *āsava*—canker: That is, as a mental effluent that pollutes the world of the mind and disturbs completely its ecological balance, brought about by wholesome states of consciousness and actions.

*Kāma* as *kilesa*—defilement: Just as rust, arising from iron, eats into it and destroys it, even so *kāma* as a mental corrosive defiles, corrupts and pollutes the mind.

*Kāma* as *ogha*—flood: Just as a flood inundates and engulfs whatever lies on its way, even so, sense-desire overwhelms the mind, completely holds it under its sway and engulfs it.

*Kāma* as *yoga*—bond: Signifying how desire, by yoking the mind in sensuous enjoyment, keeps it perpetually in thraldom or bondage. Here, the word *yoga* also means application, implying thereby how, under the influence of *kāma*, the mind tends to apply itself to the gratification of sensual desires.

*Kāma* as *abhijjhā-kāyagantha*, is the tie of covetousness that binds the mind with the body. That is to say that desire, as covetousness, is a tie that binds the mind and body in a manner a waist-band holds the apparel tightly. The term *kāya* literally meaning 'body' here implies both the physical and the mental bodies *(rūpakāya, nāmakāya)* in the sense of aggregates. The tie of desire—coveting, yearning or hankering unrelentingly—holds the mind in its grip, in a state of perpetual slavery.

*Kāma* as *upādāna*—clinging: when sense-desire, in the form of craving, gets intensified and accentuated through repetition, it grows into a mental clinging or attachment that seizes onto the object, arousing passion, lust or greed, in the way a leech clings on to and sucks blood. It is this sensual clinging or attachment that is at the root of an unwholesome *kamma*, which involves one in the *vaṭṭa*, the vicious circle of becoming (*bhava*).

*Kāma* as *nīvaraṇa*—hindrance: that is, sensual desire as an impediment to the progress of the mind, in the way a road-block obstructs all movement or communication. Because it is a mental obstacle *kāma* is called *kāmacchanda*—sensuality, a prepossessing urge which, by overtaking, hinders the mind from evolving as progressing.

*Kāma* as *kilesa*—defilement: Just as rust, arising from iron, eats into it and destroys it, even so *kāma* as a mental corrosive defiles, corrupts and pollutes the mind.

*Kāma* as *ogha*—flood: Just as a flood inundates and engulfs whatever lies on its way, even so, sense-desire overwhelms the mind, completely holds it under its sway and engulfs it.

*Kāma* as *yoga*—bond: Signifying how desire, by yoking the mind in sensuous enjoyment, keeps it perpetually in thraldom or bondage. Here, the word *yoga* also means application, implying thereby how, under the influence of *kāma*, the mind tends to apply itself to the gratification of sensual desires.

*Kāma* as *abhijjhā-kāyagantha*, is the tie of covetousness that binds the mind with the body. That is to say that desire, as covetousness, is a tie that binds the mind and body in a manner a waist-band holds the apparel tightly. The term *kāya* literally mean 'body' here it implies both the physical and the mental bodies *(rūpakāya, nāmakāya)* in the sense of aggregates. The tie of desire—coveting, yearning or hankering unrelentingly—holds the mind in its grip, in a state of perpetual slavery.

*Kāma* as *upādāna*—clinging: When sense-desire, in the form of craving, gets intensified and accentuated through repetition, it grows into a mental clinging or attachment that seizes onto the object, arousing passion, lust or greed, in the way a leech clings on to and sucks blood. It is this sensual clinging or attachment that is at the root of an unwholesome *kamma*, which involves one in the *vaṭṭa*, the vicious circle of becoming (*bhava*).

*Kāma* as *nīvaraṇa*—hindrance: that is, sensual desire as an impediment to the progress of the mind, in the way a roadblock obstructs all movement or communication. Because it is a mental obstacle *kāma* is called *kāmacchanda*—sensuality, a prepossessing urge which, by overtaking, hinders the mind from evolving or progressing.

*Kāma* as *saṃyojana*—fetter: sense-desire as *kāma-rāga*—passion, is a fetter. Passion colours the mind (*rañjeti*), *i.e.*, conditions it totally, influences it like an intoxicant, infatuates it like a bee that is drowned in honey; the mind thus thoroughly caught up and imprisoned, loses all sense of judgement and freedom, hence the metaphor of a 'fetter'.

*Kāma* as *anusaya*—latent tendency: that is, desire as a dormant disposition. With the slightest perturbation it gets activated, even as a man who sleeps lightly, with the slightest noise, wakes up. This latency only underlines its potency, its insidious capacity. Just as a plant, with well-established roots, even if cut off repeatedly sprouts, even so, *kāmānusaya* gives rise to unwholesome thoughts whenever the mind is 'inclined to enjoy' a pleasurable object.

*Kāma* as *lobha-hetu*— root of greed: desire as the root of greed functions as the root of an unwholesome consciousness or action. It is this that nourishes and holds the *kilesa-vaṭṭa*—defilement-cycle which brings about the co-production of *kamma-vaṭṭa*—action cycle, which in turn results in *vipāka-vaṭṭa*—the resultant-cycle, thus perpetually rotating the wheel of recurring existence.

Because of this perennial quality of *kāma*, as evident from the aforesaid terms, sense-desire, both as a subjective and as an objective relation mutually interacting, preserves and perpetuates existence as a unending involvement.

The Buddha used some very expressive figures of speech to bring home the truth about *kāma*—sensuality. In the *Bhaya Sutta* (*AN*. VI, 23), he described *kāma* as a synonym of 'fear', 'suffering', 'disease', 'abscess', 'bond', and 'bog'. In the *Alagaddūpama Sutta*, (*MN*. 22) *kāma* has been likened to a skeleton, a lump of flesh, a grass-torch, a pit of glowing embers, a dream, a borrowed article, a fruit in the tree, a slaughter-house, an impaling stake and a snake's head. In the Vinaya *kāma* has been depicted by a very telling analogy of the itch (*kaṇḍu*).

*Saṃsāra*, phenomenal existence, is perilous; that is why it is compared to an ocean that is fathomless, tumultuous, unending and fearsome. *Saṃsāra* stands for the truth of *dukkha*, the mass of suffering. The cause (*samudaya*) of *dukkha* is *taṇhā*, craving, a synonym of *kāma*. Craving is always accompanied by ignorance, *avijjā*, which, however, is not the cause of *dukkha*. As such, *taṇhā* or *kāma* is the real creator of this ocean of *saṃsāra*. Though *avijjā* is not the creator it is the perpetuator of *saṃsāra*, *e.g.* an *Anāgāmin* cuts off (*acchecchi*) *kāma* but not *avijjā* which only an *Arahat* destroys. Owing to its all-pervasive and primeval grip over the mind *kāma*, indeed, is fearful.

Just as fever brings suffering through its abnormal symptoms, even so *kāma*, as the fever of sensuality, is suffering. The phrases 'fever of sensuality,' and 'the illness of passion', frequently found in the Pāli Canon, are reflective of the abnormal and unhealthy condition of the disease of *kāma*, which is not only an affliction, but is more as a pain-laden misfortune as when one gets a carbuncle. *Kāma* incarcerates one in the prison-house of the triple-*vaṭṭa*—the cycle of defilements, actions and resultants. And *kāma* indeed is filthy and ugly, and into this one falls as if in to a bog.

The simile of the skeleton is exceedingly appropriate, not only as the repulsive frame of the human body but also as something basically deceptive and frustrating. As an illustration there is the story of the dog, who mistook the bone to be meat and chewed on only to be frustrated. *Kāma* is insidious, it ensnares by its deceptively attractive qualities. Therefore, said the Buddha, "Indeed, sensuality is of little satisfaction but of much pain and much tribulation, with frightening consequences (*appassādā kāmā bahudukkhā bahupāyāsā ādinavo ettha bhiyyo*).

The simile of the lump of flesh, according to the commentary, illustrates one great truth that the human body is shared by many others (*bahusādharaṇatthena*); it is like a commonly used dwelling, such as a public inn. Starting with very minute micro-organisms, there are literally hundreds of different types of maggots and worms, not to talk of the many pests and parasites, the germs and viruses, that share this body with us and that live on its part. The muscular structure, including the varied solid and liquid substances, that constitute the human frame and that give the appearance of beauty and thus ensnare the mind is, apart from its deceptive appearance, essentially 'un-owned', a public property, so to say.

The sense of ownership, being an egocentric possessive compulsion, is a facet of sensual desire. As soon as the insight of the common ownership, something commonly used arises, the mind undergoes an instant change for the better. The possessive and the egoistic propensities give way to an impersonal and dispassionate frame of mind. Hence the need for comprehending the 'commonly-used' simile of the lump of flesh.

The simile of the grass-torch illustrates sensuality to be causing self-injury. Its flames burn the holder's hand. Kāma, though a constituent of the mind, burns the mind itself.

The simile of the pit of glowing embers is a symbol of the fearful situation that awaits one who indulges in evil deeds, crimes etc. through *kāma*. A fire-pit strikes terror in anyone faced with the threaty being thrown into it.

The analogy of the dream meaning a 'passing show' (*ittarapaccupaṭṭhāna*), illustrates the brief and unstable nature of the pleasures that *kāma* offers. In such a context, there cannot be fulfilment or full satisfaction. The fleeting nature of sensuality ever increases or whets the hunger for it. Besides, *kāma* is said to be the well-spring of daydreams.

# Chapter 19

## UNCOVERING THE MIND

A study of the development of modern medicine is a revealing experience. The specialists, among themselves, have their own views as to which specialisation—that of the physician, the surgeon, the pathologist, the dermatologist, cardiologist etc.,—has made the maximum contribution towards the growth of modern health-care services. To the non-medical people who are open to critical assessment, it appears that surgery has made and continues to make a significant contribution to the growth of modern medicine. This has been possible because of the innumerable techniques which surgery has developed to eradicate human suffering. To the surgeon, probably, the pain is much more 'visible' than it is to others. There used to be a time when the barber was the surgeon, but it was more a carpentry on the human body that the expertise of the barber-surgeon provided.

Knowledge by itself is of little use unless it is applied, and applied positively. A technique is nothing else but practical application of knowledge. When supported by a technique, knowledge becomes a power. This is evident in the case of science and, for that matter, of humanities. In fact, what science is today is entirely because of technological application and technology means technique and method.

The Buddha broke away, for the first time in the history of religion and philosophy, from the traditional ritualistic, doctrinal and dogmatic approach. He created a spiritual technique to supplant existing rites and rituals and various superstitions, beliefs and practices. He called these techniques *pariyāya*, and by other terms like *paṭipadā*, *yāna*, *magga* and so on.

A *dhamma-pariyāya* or spiritual technique is a very specific, practical application of ethical, psychological and philosophical knowledge, which bears fruit here and now. It is a technique which brings about inner illumination and purity of life and releases one from the vicious circle of *kamma* and rebirth, and awakens in one moral, intellectual and spiritual power. The *Nibbedhika Sutta* teaches such a spiritual technique (*dhamma-pariyāya*) which, despite all forms of social changes, is ever-relevant and result-oriented.

When one methodically and skilfully puts a method into action, one is bound to achieve the desired result. This underlines the approach of *dhamma-pariyāya*, a technique which is opposed to mere theorising or blind adherence.

In the *Nibbedhika Sutta*, the Buddha enunciates the technique of penetration whereby one wisely penetrates into the mystery of one's own existence, as evident in the very day-to-day normal working of the mind. Six factors are specifically mentioned which need to be wisely penetrated. These are: sense desire, feeling, perception, canker, action and suffering. Each of these six factors is to be further subjected to a sixfold analysis. And why so? That also has to be correlated to one's life, *vis-a-vis* the goal of spiritual excellence and deliverance.

The Buddha said, "Monks, the sense-desires, should be penetrated; the conditioned origin of sense-desires should be penetrated; the variety of sense-desires should be penetrated; the result of sense-desires should be penetrated; the cessation of sense-desires should be penetrated; the path leading to the cessation of sense-desires should be penetrated. So it has been said. Why was this said?" Then he explains sense-desire to be that enjoyment-prone passion which so profoundly affects the mind of a being as to be born in a plane of existence where the desire to gratify the senses predominates.

We have here several applications of the term *kāma*—sense-desire. There is the *kāma-citta*, eight states of unwholesome consciousness rooted in greed, belonging to the sphere of sense-desire. There are also five states of consciousness known as the *ahetuka* (without root), *akusala* (unwholesome) and *vipāka citta* (resultant consciousness). These five *cittas*, based on the five sense-doors, as eye, ear, nose, tongue and body, operate on the subconscious level, being resultants of the past conscious, volitional, unwholesome actions (*kamma*). These five *ahetuka, akusala* and *vipāka* cittas are specifically meant here with reference to the first factor (sense-desire) of the *Nibbedhika Sutta*.

Then there is *kāma* as a *cetasika*—mental factor, known as *lobha*, greed, *taṇhā*, craving, *rāga*-lust, *abhijjhā*, covetousness etc. A mental factor is a concomitant of a state of consciousness. Here the analogy of a train would exemplify the relation between *citta* (consciousness) and *cetasika* (mental factor). While consciousness is like the engine, the mental factors are like the bogies, each separately constructed, with different functions. There are altogether fifty-two cetasikas, each having a different characteristic, a different function etc.

Then there is *kāma* as *kāma-guṇa*—sense objects, five in number, which are literally called the strands of sense desires because on them the desires are focused and fed and hence the mind being tied to them. These five are the external counterparts of the internal sense-organs, namely sight, sound, smell, taste and touch. The Buddha precisely delineates these *kāma-guṇas* as for instance, the sight or visible forms which are 'cognisable by eye-consciousness and are attractive, tempting, pleasing, covetable, with sensual, association and lust-producing.' Similarly it is with sound etc.

The eye, as an internal sense-faculty, reflects the sights in the manner a mirror does. It cannot cognise. Cognition is a mental action which eye-consciousness performs. Therefore, it is said to be cognisable by eye-consciousness and appears as attractive etc. Why a given sight is cognised in a way so as to produce lust or to be covetable, or with sensual association and tempting etc., is a moot point which will be discussed later. Briefly, it is upon this cognition which is desire-prone that the entire process, indicated by the other five terms and leading to suffering, depends.

Lastly, *kāma*, as already mentioned, also stands for an entire sphere of existence—*avacara* or *loka*, comprising eleven distinct planes of existence. These are the four sub-human planes called *apāya* or states of woe, one human plane, and the remaining six, the planes of gods (*devas*). In the *kāmāvacara*, beings get 'stuck' (*lubbhati*), to the objects through desire born of their senses. Actually the word 'stuck' is symptomatic of the proclivity towards the ''desire to enjoy'' (*kāmati*). Just as a fish is immersed in water, is surrounded by water, is unable to be out of water, is habituated to water, having water as the habitat, and is within the watery sphere of existence, even so is a being in the *kāma-loka*. He is entirely bound up, immersed and within the field of *kāma*, as it were and to get out of the *kāma*-habitat it requires tremendous effort, both subjectively and objectively.

Subjectively, as mentioned earlier, *kāma* as a proclivity, as a dormant proneness or inclination, as a potential force, already resides in the five types of sense-based *vipāka* consciousness, that is to say, eye-consciousness (*cakkhu-viññāṇa*), ear-, nose-, tongue-, body-consciousness. These are very subtle subconscious states which are not subject to any conscious control. At best, their existence can be inferred or seen by the mind's "hind-sight" (*paccavekkhana*). Of course, by a very sharp and acute mindfulness one can penetrate into this inherent proneness to enjoy the sense objects.

Now, how does this sense-consciousness arise? The discovery and the analysis of this exceedingly subtle working of the mind by the Buddha is an accomplishment of such rare and unique distinction, that even a highly cynical though intelligent man like the great Ionian King Menander (Milinda), had to acknowledge it in most laudatory terms, saying to the Venerable Nāgasena, the great Arahat, "Indeed, venerable Sir, the Blessed One has accomplished the wonder of all wonders by dissecting even the subtlest mental phenomena."

This is how the omniscient Buddha analysed the working of the mind based on the interaction of the sense-organs and the sense-objects: *Cakkhuñ-ca paṭicca rūpañ-ca uppajjati cakkhu-viññāṇaṃ, tiṇṇaṃ saṅgati phasso; phassa-paccayā vedanā, vedanā paccayā saññā,* "Conditioned by the eye-organ and the visible object (sight), there arises eye-consciousness, and the conjunction of these three is contact (or sense-impression); conditioned by sense-impression, there arises feeling, conditioned by feeling, arises perception." This mechanism is highly delicate, sensitive and precise. As soon as an external object comes into the focus of the sense-organ, there arises the eye consciousness (i.e., seeing or visual awareness); and the coming together of these three constitutes the mental factor called sense-impression or contact; with the arising of contact, feeling arises concurrently, as a co-nascent factor and with feeling, again perception co-exists.

And all these put together bring about *kāma* (desire-proneness), as a 'drag force' or the 'carried-over' of the past *kamma* or volitional action. A motorboat cruises fast on the placid water of a lake and the faster it moves the longer becomes the drag force, a momentum that follows in consequence of the speeding boat. If the speeding boat is the *kamma* of the past, the consequential drag is the *vipāka* or resultant consciousness of the present, which arises together with the other mental factors such as sense or mental impression, feeling, perception etc., each performing its own specific task.

The 'carried-over' expression of the book-keeper is equally apt. In a double entry account book, one keeps on entering particulars of receipts and expenditures and posts the amount in the appropriate receipt and expenditure columns. When the page is fully written, all the amounts are totalled on both the columns and then carried forward to the next page again under the heads, receipt and expenditure. Then fresh particulars and figures are added thereafter.

Life is very much the same, when viewed from the angle of the law of *kamma* and rebirth. One keeps on performing volitional actions and thus keeps on accumulating *kammic* forces or energies; at the moment of death, the cumulative force of all the accumulated *kammas* conditions rebirth into a new plane, and thus gets transmitted into the new form of life. At first, the *kamma* resultants dwell as potential forces which, by coming in contact with the other appurtenances of the new existence, get activated and thereafter keep on acquiring new *kammas*. Just as the conjunction of the three, as mentioned above, is occasioned by the proneness of an inherent energy, perpetuating new volitional activities, even so, after the re-birth-linking consciousness has arisen, it is followed by a subconscious stream, called 'life-continuum' (*bhavaṅga citta),* which emerges as *ahetuka vipāka cittas* and then becomes fully conscious. Rebirth-consciousness thus lays the track of a new existence by virtue of the cumulative force of all the *kammas* of the past posited on it. The rebirth-consciousness can be compared with a warhead carrying all the nuclear force in a missile. It attracts latent *vipākas* and thereafter keeps up fresh *karmic* involvements.

To revert to the theme of the resultant five-fold sensory-consciousness, (eye-consciousness etc.), it has been mentioned that along with this *citta*, several *cetasikas* (mental factors) such as *phassa*, *vedanā*, *saññā* etc., also arise, each performing a specific function. *Phassa* fulfils a very crucial role as a psychic input that fuels (*āharati*) and helps in the origination of a specific feeling. Out of the five different types of feelings (*vedanā*) that is, *sukha* (bodily pleasant), *dukkha* (bodily painful), *somanassa* (mentally pleasant), *domanassa* (mentaly painful) and *upekkhā* (neutral), only one arises in a 'conjunction'.

What is it that determines the selection? For instance, the same object rouses very different reactions in different people; and even in the same person, an object may rouse different reactions at different times. The object being the same, it should produce an identical reaction or feeling in everybody and at all times. This does not happen. And why? Because of the potential force of the *vipāka-citta* (resultant consciousness) being varied in different people, and varied in the same person at different times.

A given *kamma* produces a certain resultant consciousness which cognises an object in a certain manner in keeping with its potential force (*samaṅgī*). Another resultant consciousness which follows this, with a very different *karmic* background, may cognise the same object, but this time differently, because of its intrinsic character, and thereby produce a different reaction or feeling. For instance, a beggar approaches several people. Some are sympathetically disposed towards him, some are hostile, and some just neutral and even the same person, who is disposed towards the beggar in a certain manner at a certain time, may be disposed quite differently at some other time. Why must the beggar rouse such varied reactions in different people, and in the same person, at different times?

Buddhist psychology would not explain it away by some obscure and untenable intellectual contrivance. The logic of this variegated response is quite obvious to an open mind. It is the work of the *vipāka citta*, that is to say, the specific *vedanā* (feeling) is determined by the potential force of the *vipāka citta*, and made functional by *phassa* (sense-impression) at the moment of the triple conjunction and in keeping with the "interpretation" given by perception (*saññā*), which also is a concomitant mental factor. Perception recognises the object in a specific manner, cognised by consciousness, and this difference of awareness is the interpretation proffered by perception, giving rise to the specificity of the feeling. This is how a psychological agglomeration fulfils a very complex task, in perfect harmony with a norm and that too, precisely. The norm referred to is the law of moral causation, otherwise called *kamma*, in the Buddha's Dhamma.

In the sacred Pāli Canon and its commentarial literature, the law of moral causation (*kamma*) has been enunciated very clearly, without ambiguity and without the irrational device of divine grace or intervention as in the case of one resorting to a supernatural element, when clarity of thought and inner perspicuity desert the mind, as is often found in the case of those advancing *kamma* as a theory or as a fatalistic belief, *e.g.* from which there is no escape except through the will of the Creator or as predestined. Fatalism and an orderly law are diametrically opposite teachings. Buddhist ethics, psychology and philosophy, have enough logical soundness to avoid subterfuges to explain away ambiguities.

The law of moral causation has been treated in terms of a mechanism that may be called circles within a circle or wheels within a wheel (*vaṭṭena vaṭṭam*). There are three circles, the *vipāka vaṭṭa*—the circle of results of *kamma*, *kilesa vaṭṭa*—the circle of mental defilements, and *kamma-vaṭṭa*—the circle of *kamma* or volitional actions. On being reborn in a particular plane of existence, one is equipped with a psycho-physical combination or body-mind mechanism. This mechanism has a certain potential force which manifests, among other things, as a proneness in a specific manner; or as an endowment of the mind or the body which cannot be reversed, in the sense that its functions are determined; but it can be profitably and wisely made use of for further evolution. For instance, the sense-faculties (eye, ear, nose, etc.) are endowments or inborn faculties, functioning with innate powers, and are inclined towards their respective objects in a specific way as already mentioned. Similarly, the mental faculties of faith (*saddhā*), energy (*viriya*), mindfulness (*sati*), concentration (*samādhi*) and wisdom (*paññā*) are inherent powers of the mind; one is born with these, but they can be sagaciously cultivated and developed.

Now, the acquired qualities represented by development, cannot come about unless there is something already present in the form of inborn endowment. The *vipāka-vaṭṭa* represents these inborn qualities, endowments etc., as the resultants of a given *kamma*. The interactions of the senses and their objects are natural, interdependent mutualities, and it would be foolish to question why they are so. Nor can this interaction be deliberately manipulated or reversed. These interactions have psychological co-essentials, as already described as the 'triple conjunction' and the complex performance of this inborn mind-mechanism is construed as *vipāka-vaṭṭa*.

When a pleasant feeling arises due to the subject-object interaction, there is the desire to enjoy the feeling. This desire in its rudimentary form is of the essence of *vipāka*. But once one begins to "taste" this feeling and delight therein, then the dormant tendency (*anusaya*) is activated, and what was a 'proclivity' now becomes an acquired 'craving'. Thus, feeling conditions craving, and craving conditions clinging and clinging in turn brings about the actual commitment of a volitional action—*kamma* (*vedanā paccayā taṇhā, taṇhā paccayā upādāna, upādāna paccayā bhava*). In other words, one thing leads to another, and yet to another, and so a chain of relations and occurrences becomes established.

While *vedanā* represents the *vipāka-vaṭṭa*, the craving for the object, induced by the feeling, represents the *kilesa-vaṭṭa*—the circle of mental defilement. Craving and clinging are mental pollutants which, arising in the mind, defile, debilitate and corrupt it. Just as industrial and urban effluents, born of the industrial and urban situation, pollute and corrode the very thing in which they are born, even so, defilement—*kilesa*, arising in the mind as active mental factors and induced by the mind's dormant inclinations or tendencies (*āsavas* as *anusayas*), pollute, weaken and corrupt the mind.

It is *kilesa* which is at the root of all evil and which fetter a being in *saṃsāra*. Now, a *kilesa* is also an *āsava*, a canker or a mental effluent. The *kilesa* operates both at the subconscious as well as at the conscious levels. There are actually three levels at which *kilesas* operate. These are

1. At the *anusaya* latent level.
2. At the *pariyuṭṭhāna* or the conscious mental level, in the form of thoughts, obsessions etc.
3. At the *vītikkama* or the action level, in the form of bodily and verbal actions.

Now, once a *kilesa* works, it simultaneously, it lays the track of *kamma* within. When a woman has conceived a child, though the child is not visible or is not actually born, it is there nonetheless. So also, with the inception of *kilesa*, that is to say, with the working of the circle of defilement (*kilesa-vaṭṭa*), the circle of *kamma* also begins to rotate. Though the *kamma* may not itself be expressed in deed or word, it is committed nonetheless mentally, and in due course its result (*vipāka*) shapes up in the same way as the child in conception, when born as a child in parturition, gives expression to the fact of conception. In other words, all these three circles or wheels—resultant (*vipāka*), defilement (*kilesa*) and volitional action (*kamma*)—are mutually dependent.

Here the analogy of the clock can be appropriately used to explain this phenomenon. Just as the 'seconds' pinion turns the 'minutes' pinion, and the 'minutes' pinion the 'hours' pinion, because all these little wheels are mutually dependent, even so are the three wheels of *vipāka*, *kilesa* and *kamma*. As the *vipāka* wheel rotates with rebirth, it also sets in motion the wheel of the *kilesa* with the subject-object interaction, and the *kilesa* wheel turns the wheel of *kamma*. Thus the wheel of becoming, with these three wheels within it, moves on and on endlessly, until it ceases with the realization of Nibbāna.

In terms of the six factors of the *Nibbedhika Sutta*, the first three factors, that is to say, sense-desires, feelings and perceptions, represent the *vipāka-vaṭṭa.* The fourth, that is, *āsava*, represents *kilesa-vaṭṭa*. The fifth, that is, *kamma*, represents the *kamma-vaṭṭa*. The last factor, that is, *dukkha*-suffering, represents life as a whole, the totality of the three circles of the Wheel of Becoming.

# Chapter 20

## ANALYTICAL APPROACH

The teachings of the Buddha can be presented in two distinct ways: Dhamma and the Abhidhamma. The former represents a popular method, which,takimg into account the realities of daily life, sets forth the teachings in conventional terms. The latter is the analytical method which, taking into account the need to decondition the mind and liberate it from *saṃsāric* bondage, sets forth the teachings from the standpoint of the ultimate reality. Whichever the way, its purpose is to reveal the truth.

The truth, according to the Buddha, is not a matter of enquiry, but of experience. The truth-equation, otherwise called the Four Noble Truths, is the core-element of the Buddha's spiritual discovery, and therefore of his teachings. This fourfold Truth or insight into reality, both of bondage (*saṃsāra*) and of liberation (Nibbāna), is essentially a spiritual experience which every seeker of truth must have. It is not a theory or a doctrine. There cannot be any misunderstanding about it. Whosoever practises the Buddha's teachings in daily life, developing moral purity, meditative concentration and intuitive insight, for him or her the truth-experience will become real. Before that, it is an intellectual knowledge which could foster self-deception. Compromises never lead to truth but assiduous effort coupled with compassion and humility does.

The teachings of the Buddha have been handed down to

us in its original form by generations of saints and illustrious teachers in the form of the sacred Pāli scriptures known as the *Tipiṭaka*—The Three Baskets. The word *piṭaka* (Basket), is a metaphor meaningfully used by the Buddha to signify the 'handing down' or 'passing on' of a live knowledge and tradition of holiness from one generation to another, in the way building materials are passed on at a construction site. Thus the *Tipiṭaka* is a guide to enlightenment (*bodhi*), to the actualisation of the Four Noble Truths. 'Basket' also signifies a collection of knowledge and experience which is to be used in the manner a blueprint is used. In other words, these three *Piṭakas, Vinaya*, *Sutta* and *Abhidhamma,* are not 'revealed' scriptures which cannot be questioned and must be blindly followed but they constitute pragmatic methods to be practised in daily life with the sole purpose of discovering the Truths, by each seeker individually.

The *Vinaya Piṭaka* is the basket of monastic discipline. The *Sutta Piṭaka* contains the discourses of the Buddha delivered through the forty-five years of an unmatched, dedicated public ministry 'for the welfare of the many, for the happiness of the many' (*bahujana-sukhāya*, *bahujana-hitāya*). These discourses, couched in ordinary day-to-day language, are exceedingly practical and edifying. They reflect the infinite wisdom and boundless compassion of the Buddha. In the *Abhidhamma Piṭaka*, the Buddha expounds his teachings strictly on philosophical terms and without recourse to popular language.

The *Abhidhamma* is entirely objective and impersonal since it enunciates from the standpoint of ultimate reality. While the first two *Piṭakas* constitute the *Dhamma*-method, as mentioned above, the last one employs the *Abhidhamma*-method—the way of higher philosophy.

So far, the *āsavas* have been treated according to the *Dhamma*-method, as enunciated in the two celebrated suttas: *Sabbāsava Sutta* (On All Cankers) and the *Nibbedhika Sutta* (Penetration). The *Abhidhamma* method, that is the analytical approach, as distinct from the conventional one, is presented in the following chapter. The basic text for this presentation is culled from the *Dhammasaṅgaṇī*, the first book of the *Abhidhamma Piṭaka*, which consists of seven books.

In this work, the *āsavas* have been treated under three headings:

1) The *āsava-gocchaka* (Canker-cluster).

2) *Nikkhepa-kaṇḍa* (Semantic exposition).

3) *Atthuddhāra-kaṇḍa* (Digest: psychological data.)

The first is a semantic analysis of the *āsavas*. The *Atthuḍdhāra-kaṇḍa*, on the contrary, contains a condensed explanation of the *cittas* or states of consciousness in which the cankers occur. It is a psychological analysis of the cankers. Because the second is a definitive, expository approach, and the third a condensed and quintessential approach, these are rendered as "exposition" and "digest" respectively.

In order to clarify the texts both of *Nikkhepa* (exposition) and *Atthuddhāra* (Digest) methods, notes have been added under the heading 'comment.'

# Chapter 21

## THE MUNDANE AND SUPRAMUNDANE

**— Table 1 —**

*Sacca* **(Truth)**

*Sammuti* - Conventional      *Paramattha* - Ultimate

(*Vinaya* & *Sutta*)      (*Abhidhamma*)

*Saṃsāra* - Five Aggregates (*Khandhas*)      *Apariyāpanna* - The Beyond (Nibbāna)

(a) 89 Cittas (states of consciousness)      (b) 52 Cetasikas (mental factors)      (c) 28 Rūpa (forms of corporeality)

1. The Buddha taught both in ordinary conventional language and in philosophical terms (Table-1). The *Vinaya* and Sutta *Piṭakas* use the conventional language, whereas the *Abhidhamma Piṭaka* is entirely impersonal and objective. The *Abhidhamma* portrays *saṃsāra*—the beings and the world—in terms of aggregates of phenomena, and the supramundane as the unconditioned element (Nibbāna).

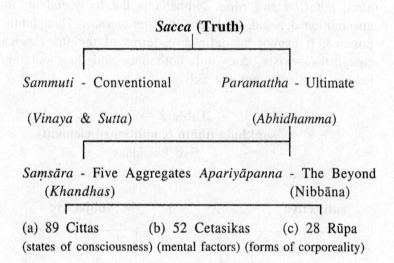

*Saṃsāra* is conditioned and as such it is the dimension of imperfection and bondage. Nibbāna is unconditioned and therefore it is the dimension of liberation. *Saṃsāra* can be reduced to psycho-physical aggregations as *citta, cetasika* and *rūpa*. There are altogether eighty-nine *cittas* or states of consciousness which, together with fifty-two *cetasikas* or mental factors, constitute mentality (*Nāma)* or mind. There are twenty-eight forms of matter or corporeality, both internal and external.

Ultimately, the whole cosmos, all that exists, from the most rudimentary to the most developed state of evolution consists, in different permutations and combinations of one hundred and sixty-nine basic elements of existence, otherwise called *citta*, *cetasika* and *rūpa*. Nibbāna is the transcendent, the unconditioned, signifying liberation from *saṃsāra*. Though most positive, it cannot be defined in terms of the four logical categories—exists, does not, both does and does not, and neither does nor does not exist.

**— Table 2 —**

**saṅkhata dhātu (conditioned element)**

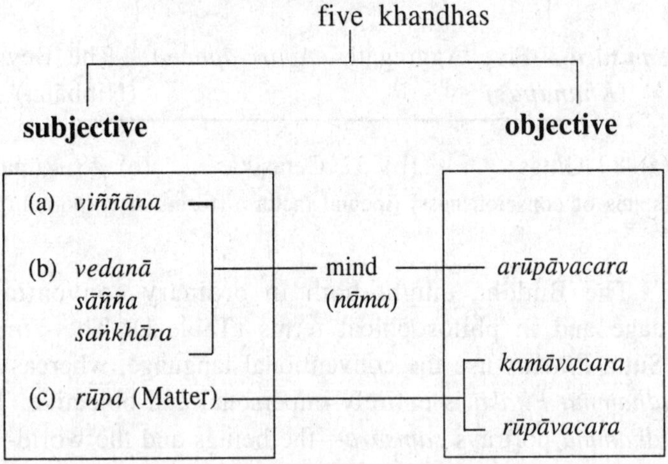


All phenomena (conditioned elements) can be ultimately reduced to the five *khandhas* (aggregates) which represent both subjective (organic) and objective (inorganic) existence. (Table-2) Subjectively, the five *khandhas* comprise the psycho-physical combination known as a being, god, man, animal, insect etc. Technically this combination is called *nāma-rūpa*. There are three distinct levels of existence known as *avacara* or *loka*. *Loka* is the external world or sphere, in which a being dwells. Both the beings and the world are thus interdependent and inseparable, signifying conditionality, otherwise called bondage. The five *khandhas* are also classified in terms of *citta*, *cetasika* and *rūpa*.

### - Table 3 -
### *Apariyapanna* (The beyond)

| subjective | objective |
|---|---|
| 1. 8 Lokuttara citta (Supramundane consciousness) | Nibbāna dhātu (unconditioned element) |
| 2. 4 Magga (path insights) | |
| 3. 4 Phala (fruition insights) | |

*Apariyāpanna* signifies that which is beyond the mundane spheres of existence and therefore above bondage and involvement in *kamma* and rebirth. *Apariyāpanna*, also called *lokuttara*, consists of eight supramundane path and fruition insights, which are attained subjectively, and of Nibbāna which is the object of these insights. The eight *lokuttara* cittas, states of insights, are accompanied by *jhāna*, meditative absorption, belonging to the five *rūpāvacara* states of consciousness. Each *jhāna* corresponds to a lokuttara path-fruition insight.

**- Table -**

| ***Lokuttara citta***<br>**(Supramundaneconsciousness)** | ***Jhāna (samādhi)***<br>**Meditative absorption** |
|---|---|
| 1.*Sotāpatti-Sakadāgāmī-Anāgāmī-Arahatta Magga and Phala*<br>The Path and Fruition Insights of Stream-Entrance-Once-Returning-Non-Returning-State of Perfection | 1. *Paṭhamajjhāna sahitaṃ*<br>Accompanied by the first stage of meditative absorption |
| 2. ------ do ------ | 2. *Dutiyaj jhāna sahitaṃ*<br>Accompanied by the second stage of meditative absorption |
| 3. ------ do ------ | 3. *Tatiyaj jhāna sahitaṃ*<br>Accompanied by the third stage of meditative absorption |
| 4. ----- do ------ | 4. *Catutthaj jhāna sahitaṃ*<br>Accompanied by the fourth stage of meditative absorption |
| 5. ----- do ------ | 5. *Pañcamaj jhāna sahitaṃ*<br>Accompanied by the fifth stage of meditative absorption |

The correlation between the supramundane path-fruition attainments and meditative absorptions, provides important clues regarding the process of enlightenment and deliverance from *saṃsāra*. The five *rūpāvacara jhānas*, meditative absorptions, are the foundations necessary for the arising of the eight *magga-phala lokuttara cittas*. When the *jhānas* are associated with the lokuttara cittas, they are transformed into the 'footholds' (*lokuttara pādaka*) for the supramundane insights. *Jhānas* are developed by *samatha* meditation, while *lokuttara magga-phala* states are developed through *vipassanā* meditation. Thus both *samatha* and *vipassanā* meditations are perfectly conjoined here forming a pair (*yuga*).

Nibbāna is the object of both the path and fruition insights, *magga-phala* ñānas. However they represent different roles and accomplishments. *Magga-ñāṇas* are the instruments for severing the fetters, therewith cessation of bondage from worldly existence. The *phala cittas* are the sublime states of absorption by which the blissful condition of Nibbāna is directly experienced. In other words while the path insight enables one to realize Nibbāna, the fruition insight enables one to enjoy the fruit of that realization. The paths are like the hands that acquire Nibbānic ambrosia, while fruitions enable one to fully savour the bliss of the ambrosia.

**- Table 5 -**

*Citta*-States of Consciousness

*viññana-khandha*
(81 *lokiya* and 8 *lokuttara* = 89)

| **type** | **level** |
|---|---|
| 1. 12 akusala | 1. 54 kāmāvacara |
| 2. 21 kusala (17 + 4) | 2. 15 rūpavacara |
| 3. 36 vipāka | 3. 12 arūpavacara |
| 4. 20 kiriyā | 4. 8 lokuttara |
| 89 | 89 |

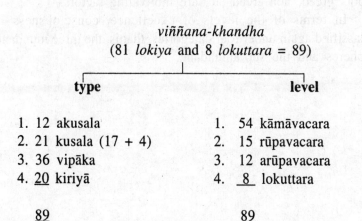

There are two distinct categories of consciousness namely, the mundane (*lokiya*) and the supramundane (*lokuttara*). While the former represents the phenomenal, which is within the sway of the cankers, and therefore of bondage and endless becoming, the latter belongs to the dimension of the Beyond (*apariyāpanna*), a transformed state transcending in stages the range of the cankers and therefore out of the vicious circle of *saṃsāra*.

In terms of their intrinsic nature, the eighty-one *lokiya-cittas* belong to four different types, the unwholesome (*akusala*), rooted in greed, hatred and delusion; the wholesome (*kusala*), rooted in non-greed, non-hatred and non-delusion; the indeterminate (*abyākata*), comprising the resultant (*vipāka*) and the functional (*kiriya*). It is called *abyākata* because it is neither wholesome nor unwholesome, but the results thereof, known as *vipāka*, as also purely functional (kriyā) which is neither good nor bad, nor their resultants.

Good and bad, therefore, are not conventional notions, but psychological realities. In Buddhism, ethics or morality is thus based on *paramattha* (ultimate) values, and is not the creature of convention, scripture, jurisprudence and such devices. The roots greed, non-greed etc. are motivating factors.

In terms of the levels of excellence, consciousness is classified again under four categories, that is, the three mundane spheres and the supramundane.

**- Table 6 -**

**12 *Akusala citta* (unwholesome consciousness)**

| | | |
|---|---|---|
| | Rooted in greed (*lobha-mūlika*) | |
| 1. | Joyful with wrong view | - spontaneous |
| 2. | Joyful with wrong view | - induced |
| 3. | Joyful without wrong view | - spontaneous |
| 4. | Joyful without wrong view | - induced |
| 5. | Indifferent with wrong view | - spontaneous |
| 6. | Indifferent with wrong view | - induced |
| 7. | Indifferent without wrong view | - spontaneous |
| 8. | Indifferent without wrong view | - induced |
| | Rooted in hatred (*dosa-mūlika*) | |
| 9. | Depressed with resentment | - spontaneous |
| 10. | Depressed with resentment | - induced |
| | Rooted in delusion (*moha-mūlika*) | |
| 11. | Indifferent with skeptical doubt | |
| 12. | Indifferent with restlessness | |

***Kāmāvacara:* associated with cankers**

*Kāmāsava* - 8 *lobha-mūlika* (rooted in greed)

*Bhavāsava* - 4 *diṭṭhi-vippayutta* (without false view)

*Ditthāsava* - 4 *diṭṭhi-sampayutta* (with false view)

*Avijjāsava* - all the 12 *akusala*

Though the unwholesome states are determined by the roots (*hetu*), they are to be understood also in terms of the cankers for a clear grasp of the phenomenon of evil, the dark, de-meritorious mental factors. Greed-rooted consciousness, accompanied by conceit and wrong view, harbours *bhavāsava* and *diṭṭhāsava*, while *kāmāsava* obtains in all the eight *lobha-mūlikas*. *Avijjāsava* is the common factor in all the twelve *akusala-cittas*.

It is interesting to note that while hatred (*dosa*) is a root (*hetu*), it is not an *āsava*, unlike the two other *hetus*, *lobha* (= *kāma*) and *moha* (= *avijjā*), which are both *hetus* and *āsavas*. This difference is to be understood in terms of the functions of these factors. *Lobha* and *moha* are the primordial twins which, like a perennial river, keep going the flow of the psycho-physical continuum otherwise called life. On the other hand, *dosa*, like an aberration, is an irregularity, a transgression. Like fire, it flares up and subsides, burning off the fuel which feeds it. It does not allow any continuity, unlike *lobha* and *moha*, which are characterised by self-sustenance.

To use a modern analogy, *lobha* and *moha* possess a homeostatic mechanism, a feedback system, with a self-regulatory and self-generative operation. The study of *āsavas*, thus, provides a wonderful insight into the cybernetics of mind. In other words, since the *hetus—lobha* and *moha*—forming the passive aspect of the personality as character-traits (*vipāka*), act back upon the causes, (*taṇhā* = *kāmāsava* and *avijjāsava*), forming the active aspect as present *karmic* patterns, a feedback mechanism is established, ensuring a perennial flow of the *āsavas*. However *dosa* does not establish a feedback system. It is irregular, characterised by force, eruption and disruption; it works in spurts and it does not act as a flow. It is not an effluent, as in the case of an *āsava*.

In a dichotomous world, there is always a tendency for the mind to swing between opposites. That is how a greed-rooted consciousness has the tendency to swing to the other extreme, namely, the hate-rooted consciousness. In day-to-day experience, this fact is very evident. If one desires something and it is not satisfied, frustration sets in, resentment grows, and a number of other antipathetic emotions arise. The common link between these two extreme mental conditions is *moha*—delusion. This fluctuating pattern is ultimately the ground for the arising and perpetuation of the unwholesome states, in particular the cankers.

**- Table 7 -**
**Kusalābyākata**
**(Wholesome and indeterminate consciousness) dissociated from cankers**

| | ***Kusala*** **Wholesome** | ***Abyākata*** **Indeterminate** ***Vipāka*** **Resultant** | ***Abyākata*** **Indeterminate** ***Kiriya*** **Functional** | **Total** |
|---|---|---|---|---|
| **1. *Kāmāvacara*** | **8** | **23** | **11** | **42** |
| **2. *Rūpāvacara*** | **5** | **5** | **5** | **15** |
| **3. *Arūpāvacara*** | **4** | **4** | **4** | **12** |
| **4. *Lokkuttara*** | **4** | **4** | **-** | **8** |
| **Total** | **21** | **36** | **20** | **77** |

The *Dhammasaṅgaṇī* contains an enumeration of Dhammas—both *lokiya* and *lokuttara*—in accordance with the *tīkā* and *duka-mātikā*—triad and duad schemata. The first of the triads is known as *kusalattika*—the wholesome triad. It is an arrangement by which everything—mundane and supramundane—is analysed under these three heads: *kusala* (wholesome), *akusala* (unwholesome) and *abyākata* (indeterminate). *Abyākata* includes *vipāka* (resultant) and *kiriya* (functional) *-cittas*, *rūpa* (matter) and Nibbāna. The *akusala-cittas* have been already mentioned. *Kusala* and *abyākata cittas* are dealt with here.

There are altogether twenty-one *kusala-cittas* belonging to all the three *lokiya* (mundane) spheres, and to the *lokuttara*, which consists of the four path-insights (*magga-cittas*). There are two distinct types of *kusala-cittas*: one is known as *ñāṇa-vippayutta* (dissociated from insight), and the other as *ñāṇa-sampayutta* (associated with insight). The former consists of four states of consciousness pertaining to the *kāmāvacara*, and the latter, of the remaining seventeen. That there are only four *kusalas* without *ñāṇa* is an interesting point; for, goodness by itself, without wisdom, only means perpetuation of the process of *kāma*, and thus *saṃsāra*, at the lowest level—*duhetuka i.e.,* birth among the unevolved humans and *asuras*. After all *kusala* also means *kamma*. Unless it is rooted in insight of a higher order, the *kamma* cannot help one to evolve in a way as to transcend all *kammas*, in the manner the *lokuttara-kusala-cittas* do.

The nine *rūpāvacara-* (fine-material sphere) and *arūpāvacara-cittas* (immaterial sphere) consciousnesses refer to states of *jhāna*—exstatic meditative absorption–which a being of the *kāmāvacara* too can develop. These sublime states of *samādhi* correspond to the consciousness of the Brahma gods, as represented by the *rūpāvacara-* and *arūpāvacara-vipākas*. The five *rūpāvacara jhāna-kusalas* also constitute the foundations necessary for the arising of the eight *lokuttara cittas*. When associated with the *lokuttara*, they are the footholds for the supramundane (*lokuttara-pādaka*). So the eight *lokuttara-cittas*, in terms of the five *jhānas*, are forty in number (8 x 5 = 40). Thus the eighty-nine *cittas*, when computed in this manner, become one hundred and twenty-one (*lokiya* 81 + *lokuttara* 40 = 121).

The eight *lokuttara cittas* arise with Nibbāna as their object. The remaining sixty-nine *cittas* (77 - 8 = 69), belonging to the three spheres, have varied mundane objects, corresponding to the six senses, that is, sight, sound etc.

The fifty-six *abyākata-cittas* are divided into thirty-six *vipāka-cittas* and twenty *kiriya-cittas*. The four *lokuttara-vipākas* are the four fruition-insights (*phala-cittas*), otherwise called *sāmañña-phalā* —fruits of recluseship, which are to be acquired by one's own spiritual excellence and effort. Out of the twenty-three *kāmāvacara vipākas*, fifteen are known as *ahetukas* (without root), and eight as *sahetukas* (with root). *Vipākas* represent the subconscious states. They constitute the subliminal substratum known as *bhavaṅga* (life continuum or lit. stream of being), with rebirth-consciousness (*paṭisandhi*) and death consciousness (*cuti*) constituting the two ends of a given life-stream. The *ahetuka-vipākas* also perform other crucial roles, technically known as the *vīthi-cittas* (lit. stations in the avenue of the mind), such as eye-consciousness, ear-consciousness etc., receiving, investigating and registering states of consciousness. A *citta*, and therewith the whole personality, is conditioned largely by these subconscious *vipāka* functions of the *vīthi* (mental process).

Out of the twenty *kiriyā-cittas*, eighteen *cittas* represent the consciousness of the canker-freed (*khīṇāsava*) Arahat, the remaining are the two functional states of advertence (*āvajjana*), both at the five-door and at the mind-door levels (*pañca-dvāra* and *mano-dvāra*). Out of the eighteen *kiriyas*, one is known as *hasituppāda*—the consciousness associated with the Arahat's smile, which is an *ahetuka* (without root) consciousness.

This special consciousness reflects the natural, effortless, cheerful mien, the bright halo of the Arahat. Though the Arahat, the Perfect One, is liberated from the bonds of *saṃsāra*, he lives like any other person, albeit for the good of the world. Since he is incapable of committing any *kamma*, his *kiriya,* functional consciousness, corresponds to the eight *kāmāvacara-kusala-cittas,* wholesome consciousness of the sphere of sense desire. This means he too can have *ñāṇa-vipayutta-cittas,* consciousness dissociated from insight, arising in his mind. The difference, however, between the ordinary person and the Arahat is that the Arahat's *ñāṇa-vipayutta-cittas* represent actions normally performed involuntarily or mechanically; that is, as a routine function, like answering the call of nature, bathing and so on. Whenever the Arahat does not bother to focus his attention deliberately on anything, and so remains unaware of certain things, such lack of concern or awareness is represented by the *ñāṇa-vipayutta-kiriyā-citta*—functional consciousness dissociated from insight.

**- Table 8 -**
**Cetasika (mental factors)**
**Co-existing with consciousness**

| | | |
|---|---|---|
| 13 aññasamāna (common factors) | 7 primary | *sabba-citta-sādhāranas* obtain in all 89 cittas |
| | 6 secondary | *pakinnakas* obtain in most cases |
| 14 *asobhana* (Morally dark or unwholesome factors) | 4 common<br>3 greed-rooted<br>4 hate-rooted<br>3 delusion-rooted | *asobhanas* occur only in the 12 *akusala cittas* |
| 25 *sobhana* (Morally bright or wholesome factors) | 19 common<br>3 *Virati*<br>2 *appamañña*<br>1 *pañña* | *sobhanas* occur in *sobhana cittas*–*kusala-vipāka,kiriya*, pertaining to *lokiya* and *lokuttara*. |
| Total 52 *cetasikas* | | |

The fifty-two *cetasikas* are concomitants of mind, factors that arise and pass away together with a state of consciousness, having the same object and the same sense-organ as the base—*ekuppāda-ekanirodha-ekālambana-vatthukā*. In other words, they are coextensive factors of the mind, built of the same stuff, so to say. Though it is essential to analyse them, identify them and penetrate into their distinctive functions for the purpose of understanding, yet, as a component coexisting with the mind, the *cetasikas* cannot be separated from the *cittas*.

There are three very distinct types of *cetasikas*: the common, the unwholesome and the wholesome factors.

The *aññasamānas* (common) are divided into primary and secondary types. The former seven are so fundamental that they are extant in all the eighty-nine *cittas*, including the ten rudimentary sense-bound *vipāka* states (*dvepañca-viññaṇa*). The six secondary *cetasikas* occur differently. They are invariably absent in the ten sense-bound *cittas*. There are other *cittas* in which some are not present, such as, the remaining *ahetuka*, the two *moha*-rooted etc.

Out of the fourteen unwholesome *cetasikas*, four are common to all the twelve *akusala cittas*. These are: *moha* (delusion), *ahirika* (lack of moral shame), *anottappa* (lack of moral fear) and *uddhacca* (restlessness). *Lobha* (greed), *diṭṭhi* (false view), and *māna* (conceit) are associated with the eight *lobha-mūlika cittas*. *Dosa* (hatred), *issā* (envy), *macchariya* (stinginess) and *kukkucca* (remorse) go together with the two *dosa-mūlika cittas*. *Thīna* (sloth) and *middha* (torpor) accompany the five *sasaṅkhārika* (induced) *cittas*. *Moha*, *vicikicchā* and *uddhacca* are conjoined with the *moha-mūlika cittas*.

It will be seen that out of the fourteen *cetasikas*, the four viz. *lobha* (=*kāmāsava*), *māna* (=*bhavāsava*), *diṭṭhi (diṭṭhāsava)* and *moha* (=*avijjāsava*) constitute the four *āsavas*. The remaining ten *cetasikas* and the twelve *akusala cittas* are associated with the *āsavas*. By functioning conjointly, they provide the *āsavas* their native environment, as it were. That is to say, the *akusala-cittas* and the ten *cetasikas* become the habitat and the haunt of the *āsavas*.

Nineteen out of the twenty-five wholesome factors are common to all *sobhana-cittas* (*sabbākusalasādhāraṇa*). The three *virati cetasikas* (abstinences) invariably go together with eight *lokuttara-cittas*. They are also found individually in the eight *kāmāvacara-kusala-cittas*. The two *appamañña-cetasikas* (*karuṇā-muditā*) are separately found in the first four *rūpāvacara-jhāna-cittas*, as also in the *kāmāvacara-kusala* and *sahetuka-kiriya-cittas*. *Paññā* arises in all *ñāṇa-sampayutta-sobhana-cittas*, pertaining to the three *lokas* and the *lokuttara*.

It is *paññā* which acts as the one sure weapon for the destruction of all the cankers, though *alobha*, as the opposite of *kāma*, counters both *kāmāsava* and *bhavāsava*. *Paññā*, as *amoha* and *sammā-diṭṭhi,* not only uproots the antipodes, *avijjāsava* and *diṭṭhāsava*, but it also destroys *kāmāsava* and *bhavāsava* already countered and attenuated by *alobha*. The nineteen *cetasikas*, including *alobha*, common to all *sobhana cittas*, make a wholesome *citta* much more powerful than an unwholesome one. That is why the good, as a positive force, has always an upper hand. However powerful the evil may appear to be, it can never withstand the good, by the very dynamics of the mind, as seen in the working of the *citta-cetasika* complex.

**- Table 9 -**
***Rūpa* (corporeality)**

**28 *rūpakkhanda***
**(Aggregate of corporeality)**

**4 primary - *suddatthaka***
**24 derived or secondary**

***Kāmāvacara*- 28**

***Rūpāvacara* - 23**
**(olfactory, gustatory, tactile, sex faculties and material group produced by nutriment, these five do not obtain)**

**21 *Kalāpas***
(Individualised clusters of matter)

| | | |
|---|---|---|
| i. *Kammaja* | - born of *kamma* | - 9 kalāpas |
| ii. *Cittaja* | - born of consciousness | - 6 kalāpas |
| iii. *Utuja* | - born of temperature | - 4 kalāpas |
| iv. *Āhāraja* | - born of nutriment | - 2 kalāpas |

*Cittaṃ, cetasikaṃ, rūpaṃ, nibbānaṃ,*
*Iti catudhā hoti paramattha-saccaṃ.*
Resolved fourfold, the Ultimate Truth is,
Consciousness, mental factor, corporeality and Nibbāna.

We have already discussed *citta* and *cetasika*. Here, the aggregate of corporeality is briefly analysed. There are twenty-eight types of corporeality, of which four are known as primary elements (*mahābhūta*), and twenty-four as derived or secondary matter. These twenty-eight kinds, both the elemental and the derived, comprise everything in the universe of matter, in all conceivable forms, organic or inorganic, gross or subtle, physical or chemical, mass or energy, visible or invisible, solid, liquid, gaseous, heat, light, electricity, magnetism, particle, wave, sight, sound, smell, taste, tangible, nutrition, vitality etc.

In terms of spheres of existence, *rūpa* belongs both to *kāmāvacara* and *rūpāvacara.* While *kāmāvacara* has all the twenty-eight kinds of matter, *rūpāvacara* has only twenty-three. This is because *rūpāvacara* does not have certain faculties like olfactory, gustatory, tactile and sex (masculinity and femininity) and nutriment born (*āhāraja*) matter. It is said, these twenty-three forms of *rūpa* which are extant in the *rūpāvacara*, also obtain in gross form in *kāmāvacara.* In other words, they are ethereal extensions of *kāmāvacara.*

There is a tremendous misconception as to the relationship between mind and matter. An intellectual materialist, a scientist, technocrat, ideologue etc. would try to make out that mind, after all, is only a tenuous or perhaps the energy-form of matter. Nothing can be more misconceived. However able and intelligent these intellectuals are, they are certainly not omniscient, and to try to pontificate on matters they do not fully understand, as their assertion that mind is but matter in energy-form, is nothing short of dogma, something tragically unscientific. According to Buddhism, mind and matter are two very disparate, dissimilar totally unlike elements, though mutually dependent and interacting under given circumstances.

While *rūpa* is *ahetuka*, rootless, without motivations, feelings, perceptions, etc., mind is not so, except the eighteen *ahetuka* states of consciousness, which are rootless in the sense of being weak, and which are accompanied by feeling, perception, volition etc. unlike matter.

The four *mahābhūtas* (primary elements) are further resolved into eight kinds of basic matter, known as *sudaṭṭhaka*, namely, *paṭhavi* (earth = solidity), *āpo* (water = liquidity), *tejo* (fire =

temperature), *vāyo* (air = motion and buoyancy), *vaṇṇa* (colour), *gandha* (smell), *rasa* (taste), *oja* (nutriment). When these eight kinds of basic matter are combined with other derived ones, they are known as units of matter (*kalāpa*). There are altogether twenty-one *kalāpas* which are born of various phenomena like *kamma*, *citta*, atmosphere and nutriment. These fourfold individualised units of matter namely *kammaja*, *cittaja*, *utuja* and *āhāraja*, consisting of twenty-one units, comprise the corporeal component (*rūpakhandha*) of the human personality.

Numerically, *kammaja-rūpa* consists of eighteen kinds, *cittaja* of fifteen, *utuja* of thirteen and *āhāraja* of twelve kinds of matter. In other words, the human body is an assemblage of fifty-eight forms of matter in different combinations and permutations, rendering the so-called personality vulnerable to innumerable dislocations and malfunctions by its very compounded structure. It is said in the *Abhidhammattha-saṅgaha* that with the arising of the rebirth consciousness, units of *kammaja* matter also arise conascently by the very power of *kamma*. This is followed by the second moment of consciousness giving rise to *cittaja-rūpas*. As the mind-matter complex thus gets established, the *utuja-rūpas* also arise and from the time nutritional essence is absorbed by the embryonic being, the *āhāraja rūpas* arise. Thus, like a flame or a river which is continuously fed, the continuity of the personality is maintained until death by the unbroken continuity of these fourfold units of matter. With the death-consciousness, *kammaja-rūpa* ceases, and thereafter *cittaja* and *āhāraja*. The *utuja-rūpas* continue till the dead body is disposed of. This immense complexity formed by the combinations and permutations of the twenty-eight primary and derived materiality in a state of flux, then, is the organic aspect (*indriya-baddha*) of *rūpa-khandha*. The inorganic materiality too constitutes a similar flow but not so complex, because of the absence of the psychological correlate. Being a compound, *rūpa* is very much conditioned and, as the object of *akusala-cittas*, as matter subject to cankers, it is essentially dissociated and disjoined from the cankers.

# Chapter 22

## Nibbāna

### - Table 10 -

### (Dimension of the unconditioned)

Nibbāna (*asaṅkhatadhātu*)

*magga* (path) — *phala* (fruition)

sacchikaranaṃ (realisation) — sukhanubhava (enjoying the bliss)

*Nirodha* (cessation) — *Vimokkha* (deliverance)

| | |
|---|---|
| 1. *Sa-upādisesa* (With *khandhas* remaining) | 1. *Suññataṃ* (voidness) |
| 2. *Anupādisesa* (Without *khandhas* remaining) | 2. *Animittaṃ* (conditionlessness) |
| | 3. *Appaõihitaṃ* (desirelessness) |

Dimension of the unconditioned

In Buddhism, the goal of all spiritual endeavour is Nibbāna. The Noble Eightfold Path, the fourth truth, stands for all spiritual endeavour. Nibbāna, the third truth, signifies the cessation of worldly bondage, and thus stands for the goal of spiritual life and the first and the second Truths, for suffering and its cause, the bondage of worldly existence. These Four Noble Truths, which the Buddha discovered and made known out of compassion for all beings, express the ultimate truths (*paramattha-sacca*) in Buddhism.

Nibbāna is called *asaṅkhata-dhātu,* the unconditioned element, in order to express its positive character. The term cessation does not mean annihilation or vanishing into nothingness. It means cessation of suffering born of worldly bondage, *saṃsāra.* Whatever is conditioned and compounded, signifies bondage, imperfection and unsatisfactoriness and as such decidedly negative. Contrarily, the unconditioned signifies freedom, perfection, happiness and excellence, wherefore it is pre-eminently positive. Because it is most positive and exalted, Nibbāna the unconditioned, is the true and the highest goal. Thus, Nibbāna is the object of the supramundane states of consciousness (*lokuttara*), which transforms the mind from the mundane to the supramundane.

Nibbāna is the object of both the path and the fruition-insights, the *magga* and the *phala cittas.* However, they stand for different roles and accomplishments. The *magga-cittas* are the instruments for severing the fetters, therewith cessation of the bondage of worldly existence. And *phala -cittas* are those sublime states of absorptions by which the blissful condition of Nibbāna is directly experienced. In other words, while the Path insight enables one to realize Nibbāna, the fruition insight enables one to enjoy the fruit of realization. The paths are like the hands that reach for and win the Nibbānic ambrosia, while the fruitions enable one to fully savour the bliss of the ambrosia.

There are two distinct types of realisation of Nibbāna. One, *sa-upādisesa*, with the psycho-physical combination called life still intact, and the other *anupādisesa*, without the *khandhas*, that is, at the final dissolution of life, as when an Arahat finally passes away (*parinibbāna*), no more to be reborn in any sphere of existence. In other words, so long as the Arahat lives, he lives in the enjoyment of the bliss of deliverance and as an exemplar for others to attain the same. The Arahats live entirely for the good of the world with the *sa-upādisesa* form of the realisation of Nibbāna.

Enjoyment of deliverance through the *samādhis* (*rūpāvacara-jhāna*) is gained by experiencing Nibbāna in three distinct forms: as Voidness, as Conditionlessness and as Desirelessness. Nibbāna is void of cankers. It is like enjoying the rarified, pure air which is void of pollution. Nibbāna is free from conditions, or signs or images; conditions signify changefulness, distraction and involvement. Freedom from these, therefore, is peace that lasts forever. Nibbāna is devoid of craving and therewith, its insatiability, pain, toil and struggle. Freedom from craving, thus, stands for the highest form of happiness and bliss.

The tasting of these threefold Nibbānic qualities is rendered possible by the development and perfection of insights into *anicca* (impermanence and changefulness), *dukkha* (suffering and toil), *anatta* (unsubstantiality and conditionedness), which characterise the dimension of bondage (*saṃsāra*). Accordingly, Nibbāna is called *anāsava*, the canker-freed dimension of the unconditioned.

In the *Udāna*, Nibbāna is described as follows, "Verily, there is an unborn, unoriginated, uncreated, unformed: if there were not this unborn, unoriginated, uncreated, unformed, deliverance from the world of the born, the originated, the created, the formed would not be possible." — *Ud* 8.3.

**Tatiya-Nibbāna-Paṭisamyutta-Sutta** *Udāna* 8.3

*Evaṃ me sutaṃ– ekaṃ samayaṃ Bhagavā sāvatthiyaṃ viharati jetavane anāthapiṇḍikassa ārāme. Tena kho pana samayena Bhagavā bhikkhū nibbānapaṭisaṃyuttāya dhammiyā kathāya sandasseti samādapeti samuttejeti sampahaṃseti. Tedha bhikkhū aṭṭhiṃ katvā, manasi katvā, sabbaṃ cetaso samannāharitvā, ohitasotā dhammaṃ suṇanti.*

*Atha kho Bhagavā etamatthaṃ viditvā tāyaṃ velāyaṃ imaṃ udānaṃ udānesi–*

*"Atthi, bhikkhave, ajātaṃ abhūtaṃ akataṃ asaṅkhataṃ.*

*No cetaṃ, bhikkhave, abhavissa ajātaṃ abhūtaṃ akataṃ asaṅkhataṃ, nayidha jātassa bhūtassa katassa saṅkhatassa nissaraṇaṃ paññāyetha. Yasmā ca kho, bhikkhave, atthi ajātaṃ abhūtaṃ akataṃ asaṅkhataṃ, tasmā jātassa bhūtassa katassa saṅkhatassa nissaraṇaṃ paññāyatī'ti.*

Translation (Discourse on Parinibbāna)

"Thus have I heard. Once the Blessed one was staying at Anāthapiṇḍika's monastery in Jeta's Grove near Sāvatthī. At that time the Lord was instructing the bhikkhus with a Dhamma-teaching related to Nibbāna, rousing them, inspiring and gladdening them. Those bhikkhus, being earnest and attentive, with their minds fully focused, were intent on hearing the teaching (Dhamma).

Then, being fully aware of its significance, on that occasion the Blessed One breathed forth this inspired utterance:

"Bhikkhus, indeed, there is an unborn, unoriginated, uncreated, unconditioned. Bhikkhus, if there were not this unborn, unoriginated, uncreated, unconditioned escape from the world of the born, the originated, the created, the conditioned would not be feasible. But because there is an unborn, unoriginated, uncreated, unconditioned, therefore an escape is feasible from the world of the born, the originated, the created, the conditioned."

# Chapter 23

## The Cluster of Cankers

*Dhammasaṅgaṇī* 3. 1. 36 & 4. 2. 36
(Translated by Venerable Acharya Buddharakkhita)

Exposition (*Nikkhepa*)

Which mental factors are cankers?

There are four cankers, namely, canker of desire for sense-pleasure, the canker of desire for the continuation of existence, the canker of wrong views, the canker of ignorance.

a) There, what is the canker of desire for sense-pleasure?

That sensual desire, the lust for sensual gratification, the delight in sensuality, the craving for sense-pleasures, the carnal love, the fever of passion, the infatuation with sensuous enjoyments, the holding on to objects of the senses—this is called the canker of desire for sense-pleasure.

b) There, what is the canker of desire for the continuation of existence?

That desire for the continuation of existence, the lust for, the delight in, the craving and the love for, the fever of, the infatuation with, and the holding on to existence, in the various planes of existence—this is called the canker of desire for the continuation of existence.

c) There, what is the canker of wrong view?

That the world is eternal, or that it is not eternal; that the world is finite, or that it is infinite; that the soul is the body, or that soul is different from the body; that the Bearer of Truth (Tathāgata) exists after his death, or that the Bearer of Truth does not exist after his death, or that the Bearer of Truth, both exists and does not exist after his death, or that the Bearer of Truth neither exists nor does not exist after his death—this kind of wrong view, this holding of a wrong religious creed, this thicket of perverse understanding, this wilderness of wrong belief, this twisted faith-pattern, this wrangling over wrong ideology, this fetter of perverted view, this dogmatic grip, this tenacious wrong persuasion, this fanatical fixation, this wrong adherence to a dogma, this blind alley, this misleading path, this falsehood, this bigoted belief, this distorted grasp (of actuality)—this is called the canker of wrong views.

d) There, what is the canker of ignorance?

The non-comprehension of (the truth of) suffering, the non-comprehension of (the truth of) the cause of suffering, the non-comprehension of (the truth of) the cessation of suffering, the non-comprehension of (the truth of) the path leading to the cessation of suffering, the non-comprehension of the past (lives), the non-comprehension of the future (lives), the non-comprehension of both the past and the future (lives. *i.e.,* as related to present life), the non-comprehension of the law of moral causation, namely, the dependent origination of the conditions supporting life, this kind of non-comprehension, this non-seeing, this non-understanding, this non-awakening, this non-enlightenment, this non-penetration, this non-grasping, this dim-wittedness, this absence of wisdom, this lack of insight, this delusion, this stupidity, this obtuseness, this ignorance, this flood of ignorance, this bond of ignorance, this predisposition of ignorance, this barrier of ignorance, this obstruction of ignorance, this delusion, this root of evil—this is called the canker of ignorance.

These are the factors that are cankers.

**Digest** (*atth'uddhāravasena*)

Which factors are cankers?

There are four cankers, namely, the canker of desire for sense-pleasure, the canker of desire for the continuation of existence, the canker of wrong views, the canker of ignorance.

The canker of desire for sense-pleasures arises in the eight states of consciousness rooted in (lit. accompanied by) greed.

The canker of desire for the continuation of existence arises in the four greed-rooted states of consciousness that are unaccompanied by wrong views. The canker of wrong views arises in the four greed-rooted states of consciousness that are accompanied by wrong views.

The canker of ignorance arises in all the (twelve) unwholesome states (of consciousness).

These factors are cankers.

**Comment**

It would have been noticed that the word 'there' (Pāli—*tattha*) occurs while defining the four *āsavas* under the heading 'Exposition'. This emphasises the contextual usage of the words. It has been already mentioned that while *nikkhepa-khaṇḍa* provides the semantic analysis, *atth'uddhāra* covers the psychological implications. Contextually, sensual desire (*kāmāsava*) boils down to a compulsion (desire, lust, gratification, craving, delight etc.) which is excited by the objects of the senses. This means a subject-object relationship, a mutual attraction, working automatically, so to say, at every level, whether latent or activated. The Pāli word for this compulsion is *ajjhosāna*, which is derived from the root 'to bind' (*adhi* + *ava* + √*sā* = *sayati* = to bind). *Kāmāsava*, then, signifies a psychological factor which is bent on, or inclined to the objects of the senses. In other words, it is the tendency to cleave to, hold on or get stuck to the objects. The senses and the sense objects are, so to say, glued together, since *kāmāsava* creates the urge to cleave to sensuous things.

*Bhavāsava*, too, is characterised by the same tendency to cleave to, but then the object this time is to continue to exist. The survival-compulsion, thus, is the essence of *bhavāsava*. What exactly is the compulsion or instinct for survival? The answer is very clearly given in the Digest-section. It is said that while *kāmāsava* arises in the eight *lobha-mūlika* (greed-rooted) *cittas* (consciousness), *bhavāsava* arises only in the four *diṭṭhi-vippayutta* (unaccompanied by perverse views) *cittas*, which are also greed-rooted. The implication is that since the four *cittas* have *māna* (conceit) as the basic drive, the survival-compulsion essentially is a struggle of the self to survive., In other words, egocentricity is the moving force underlying *bhavāsava*. It is also said in the texts that this cleaving to life refers to various planes of existence. The implication is again that life and the external world, as such, are inseparable conditions, they are mutually interdependent. Self-conceit, or the notion of 'I' or 'mine', as a separate entity belonging to a sphere, is that primordial compulsion which is responsible for an individual's recurring existence, *saṃsāra*. Rebirth, even in the higher and most blissful planes of the Brahma gods and the various heavenly realms, is brought about by this persisting, perennial and primitive sense of ownership and belonging.

The *Abhidhamma* also enumerates three distinct modes of egocentricity, viz., *seyya-māna*—superiority-conceit, *sadisa-māna*—equality-conceit and *hīna-māna*—inferiority-conceit. Any student of psychology will see that this is a much more advanced, accurate and comprehensive definition of ego than what modern psychology purports to make out with its circumscribed concept of the complex—inferiority and superiority. A separative consciousness, by its very nature, craves for recognition, and this means not only a superior status, but also very much an equal status or an inferior one. A racist, a higher caste or communal-minded individual, feeds his superiority-conceit not only with the notion of being superior, but also as a nature or divine-endowed, privileged entity which must be continued from life to life, and in the various modes of existence. Societal factors are thus closely connected with the sense of privilege originating from the extraneous agency due to one's notion of individual superiority.

The politician, the scientist in particular, the communists and the socialists who are given to the concept of an egalitarian society and equality of all kinds, suffer from equality-conceit. Members of minority communities or the socially and economically downtrodden and depressed classes, in order to enjoy various privileges, also develop a vested interest in their otherwise inferior and exploited status. It is like somebody trying to extract sympathy and compassion because of disability, age, sex, etc. Whatever is the nature of the conceit — superiority, equality, inferiority—its basic quality is the same, namely, a compulsion for recognition.

The canker of wrong view—*diṭṭhāsava*—has been defined elaborately, with the connotations very clearly spelt out, so that *māna* and *diṭṭhi* are not confused. Basically, *diṭṭhāsava* is an ideological fixation or a belief-pattern. The preoccupation with certain views connected with religious or secular creeds like communism, socialism, capitalism, free-market enterprise, etc., and with theoretical science, constitutes the breeding ground for these ideological fixations. Whether the world is eternal, finite or otherwise, whether there is a soul in the body or otherwise, whether the Tathāgata (the Bearer of Truth, a term which the Buddha used to refer to himself,) continue to exist after his Parinibbāna (final decease), or otherwise—these are purely metaphysical speculations, unsupported by realities. Nobody can prove or disprove them and they invariably end up as intellectual gymnastic, or worse, as dogma. The Ultimate

Reality (Nibbāna) transcends all the four categories of logic—is, is not, both is and is not, and neither is nor is not. After the Buddha had attained the final passing away (Mahāparinibbāna), to speculate whether he continues to exist, whether he does not exist, or whether he exists and does not exist at the same time, or whether he neither exists nor does not exist at the same time, simply is muddled-thinking, which is worse confounded by dogmatism and self-opinionatedness. To say that the Buddha exists after his final decease amounts to the eternalistic perversion of reality (*sassata-diṭṭhi*). It means that the Buddha still is trapped within the ambit of the threefold *loka*, and has not achieved deliverance. Even if the Buddha is given the trappings of an exalted Divinity or God, the absurd premise of his being unliberated and unenlightened cannot be avoided. The word Buddha itself stands for a Liberated and Enlightened One.

Contrarily, to say that the Tathāgatha does not exist, amounts to nihilism, the materialistic dogma which says that after death everything is finished, that there is no such thing as *kamma* and rebirth, or liberation from *kamma* and rebirth, etc., a position diametrically opposed to that of Buddhism. Similarly, to dub the Buddha's *parinibbāna* as the two remaining categories of logical absurdities would be equally distorted.

Speculative views of this nature, including the soul-theory as found in the *Sabbāsava Sutta* in terms of the three periods of time past, future and present—I was, I was not, etc., I will be, will not be, etc., I am, I am not, etc., —are exercises in futility rooted in a distorted grasp of actuality. Self-illusion (*sakkāya diṭṭhi*) is the mental fixation of individualism. Though it has elements akin to egotism, it is not ego or conceit as such. While conceit is a form of craving for recognition and reward, self-illusion, on the contrary, is a distorted or twisted view which grows into a perverse understanding, leading to a faith-pattern, an ideology, persuasion, sectarian, or fanatical creed. *Diṭṭhi*, therefore, has been very aptly described as a thicket, a wilderness, a wrangling, a blind alley etc. In essence, it is a distorted vision of reality which is very different from craving or gratification etc.

Conceit has the appetitive element, while wrong view has the quality of beclouding and distorting the mental view and thereby, reality, which is the object of the view. It is like the optical illusion which misconstrues a stretch of burning sand to be an expanse of cool, blue water. In the Digest section, the canker of wrong view has been summarised as the factor which arises in the four greed-rooted consciousness that are accompanied by wrong view. Thus, out of the eight states of greed-rooted consciousness, the four states which are accompanied by *māna* constitute the habitat for *bhavāsava*, the four accompanied by *diṭṭhi*, for *diṭṭhāsava* and all the eight *lobha-mūlika cittas* harbour *kāmāsava*.

The canker of ignorance is the most pervasive and deep-rooted of all cankers, as is clear from the definition given in the Digest-section, *viz.*, "The canker of ignorance arises in all the twelve unwholesome states of consciousness." Basically, it signifies mental blindness, both as non-comprehension and as delusion. The inability to grasp the realities of life and the world around, and the Transcendent (Nibbāna), as well as, the Path leading to it, implies a serious disability and a defective mechanism. It's like a physically handicapped person whose disabilities arise from the defective nature of his body. The delusion-aspect of ignorance signifies the erroneous and faulty comprehension in consequence of the defective nature of the mechanism of the mind. It's like the handicapped man doing things in such a clumsy and wrong way as to render his actions self-defeating and self-destructive. So, *avijja-āsava* means, not only not knowing, but also knowing wrongly so as to make knowledge dangerous. Wars, exploitations and a myriad other forms of inhuman and evil acts, arise mostly from the misuse of knowledge.

It is interesting to know that *avijjāsava* arises in all the twelve *akusala-cittas*. In the eight *lobha-mūlika-cittas*, it acts, in the manner of a senior partner, conjointly with *kāma*, *bhava* and *diṭṭhi-āsavas*. Because the *lobha-mūlika cittas* have three *āsavas* in different combinations, they have wide-ranging and fundamental roles in the continuity of *saṃsāra*, i.e. the process of becoming and bondage. In the two *dosa-mūlika cittas* and the two *moha-mūlika-cittas*, *avjjjā* is the only *āsava*. Though numerically single, by virtue of its potency, the two hate-rooted and the two delusion-rooted states of consciousness are destructive enough. The *dosa-mūlika cittas* are like the well-spring of all forms of sorrow in the world. The two *moha-mūlika cittas* are indeed sinister due to the darkness with which they enshroud the mind. Mental fragmentation or restlessness, cynicism or doubt, are the ominous products of this condition of blindness.

The mind wanders and is fickle. It is subject to distraction and discursiveness because of a built-in inadequacy and debility. The mind wanders or it is restless because it is unsteady and weak. Whatever is unsteady and weak is inadequate and is prone to all sorts of diseases and perils. This inadequacy and debility is the handiwork of the canker of ignorance. Ignorance is made out to be a negative condition as the absence of knowledge. This is not true. Ignorance, indeed, is a very positive *i.e.,* operative condition. Obtuseness, stupidity, not awakening to truth, inability to see through, not understanding or comprehending—these are positive, active factors.

Not knowing what one was in the past life, or inability to know what one is going to be in the future, or even after an hour, is a real handicap. The fact that by cultivating insight and wisdom which is a superior, positive condition, one can certainly overcome ignorance is enough proof of this contention.

The argument that ignorance means 'not knowing of the four Noble Truths' and not the 'not knowing of the past and future', misses the vital point that knowledge of the past, in the sense of recalling past lives (Pubbenivāsānussati), is a part of the insight into the law of kamma and rebirth. As such, it is a part of the Noble Truth of suffering (dukkha) and it's origin craving (Taṇhā).

Bodhisatta Gotama developed and perfected the three vijjās, the supernormal direct knowledge and power, before he realized Nibbāna and became the Buddha Gotama.

In the first watch of the enlightenment night (between 6 and 10 p.m.) he attained the first direct knowledge and power by which he recalled all his past existences, from the time he started his mission as hermit Sumedha, till that moment. He recalled backward and forward reviewed innumerable lives with the two components of this first vijjā, namely, direct knowledge and power. The direct knowledge enabled him to clearly see and know every detail of all existences, backward and forward, while his power enabled him to recall the past lives.

In the second watch (between 10 p.m. and 2 a.m.), he developed and perfected the second direct knowledge and power, namely, Dibbacakkhu, divine vision, enabling him to see through others' evolutionary processes, life after life, and the underlying causes thereof. The two components of this vision, 1.Cutūpapāta abhiññā, the power and knowledge of seeing deaths and rebirths of sentient beings; 2. Yathā kammūpaga abhiññā, the power and knowledge of seeing through the underlying causes, which are meritorious or demeritorious volitional activities (kamma).

This profound insight into the kammic background of his own evolutionary processes and that of other sentient beings, enabled him to foresee the future destinies of sentient beings (Anāgataṃsa ñāṇa), based on the accumulated kammic formations of good and bad deeds of past and present existences. By perfecting these two vijjas, the Bodhisatta's mind was now fully empowered to acquire the third and crucial vijjā called Āsavakkhaya ñāṇa, destruction of mental cankers, in the third watch of the night (between 2 a.m. and 6 a.m.) leading to the attainment of Supreme Enlightenment (Sambodhi).

Thus knowledge of the past and future is part of knowledge of Four Noble Truths.

The Exposition-section defines this canker to be a barrier, a root-condition and a flood, only to highlight the positive or absolute character of ignorance, in the sense that it actually exists, though unwholesome, and that it is not a mere relative factor, that is, it does not exist by itself but is visible because of the existence of something else. In other words, the canker of ignorance is characterised by the fact of the presence of bondage in *saṃsāra*, by the subjection to *kamma* and repeated rebirth, and not merely by the absence of liberation and wisdom.

**Exposition**:

Which factors are non-cankers?

Except the aforesaid factors, (i.e., cankers), the remaining wholesome, the unwholesome and the indeterminate states pertaining to the sphere of sense desire, the sphere of subtle form, the immaterial sphere and the supramundane (lit. beyond the ambit of the mundane sphere); the aggregates of feelings, perceptions, mental formations and consciousness; all corporeality, and the unconditioned element (Nibbāna)—these are the factors that are non-cankers.

**Digest:**

Which are the factors that are non-cankers?

Except the cankers and the remaining unwholesome states (of consciousness and their concomitants), the wholesome states pertaining to the four spheres, the resultant states pertaining to the four spheres, the functional-indeterminate states pertaining to the three spheres, corporeality, and Nibbāna—these are the factors that are non-cankers.

**Comment**

The Exposition and Digest methods can be reduced to these three classifications:

i. The subjective realities—*cittā-cetasikā dhammā, kusala, akusala, abyākata,* (=*vipāka, kiriya, rūpa, Nibbāna*).

ii. The objective realities *i.e.,* the spheres of existence, *kāma*, *rūpa*, *arūpa lokas* and *apariyāpanna*.

iii. The *five khandhas: rūpa,vedanā, saññā, saṅkhārā* and *viññāṇa*, i.e., in terms of the conditioned phenomena, and the unconditioned.

The principle underlying these classifications is to portray life in its bare truths that is to say, from the standpoint of Ultimate Reality and as distinct from conventional requirements. This pattern of the presentation is typical of the *Abhidhamma*, the underlying purpose being to turn knowledge into an experience.

"So long as knowledge remains just a bank of information, it hardly affects the personality. Only when it is translated into an experience, it further grows into a transforming element in the form of supramundane insights. Mere analysis of the personality in terms of the above three classifications can degenerate into an intellectual exercise. However, when one uses this knowledge as part of the *vipassanā*—insight exercises, which is what *Abhidhamma* is meant for, it is then that the wealth of this bank is utilised to bring about transformation of the personality.

The non-canker is both mundane and supramundane. What enables it to include all these wholly dissimilar states? What is it that characterizes a non-canker? Is it just the absence of a canker?

A non-canker can be construed as that which does not produce a self-sustaining mechanism or a feedback system in a way as to put something into bondage and to perpetuate bondage. The supramundane, as a liberating agency (insight), as well as a dimension of liberation (Nibbāna), negates bondage; it dries up the perennial river of the *āsavas*. Therefore it is non-canker.

The *kusalas* and *abyākatas*, too, are non-cankers, because they ward off and overcome cankers. The twelve *akusala cittas* as well as the ten *cetasikas* conjoined therewith are non-cankers, because they are merely associates of *āsavas*, and they only provide the native environment for the *āsavas* to grow. It is to be understood that *āsava* is *āsava* by virtue of a certain function, namely, its capacity to establish a feedback mechanism. The non-*āsavas* don't function this way. Therefore they are non-cankers, and not just because they signify the absence of *āsavas*.

*Avijjā* and *taṇhā* are the eternal twins that together form the primordial progenitors of all that exists. They lay ahead the track of *saṃsāra* (recurring existence) upon which a being wanders aimlessly and endlessly. Just as a pregnant woman is an evidence of a forthcoming being, even so *avijjā* and *taṇhā*, by laying the track of *saṃsāra* ensure future becoming. Until parturition the child is not visible, though pregnancy has assured its birth. The future *kamma-vipāka*, wrought by these twins, though unmanifested in the form of happiness, misery etc., yet as dormant phenomena embedded in the consciousness, are bound to get activated on maturity, in the same way the child is bound to emerge on the completion of the gestation period.

**Exposition**

Which factors are subject to (the influence of) cankers *(sāsava)*?

The wholesome, the unwholesome and the indeterminate states pertaining to the sphere of the sense desire, the sphere of subtle form, and the immaterial sphere, to wit, the aggregates of feelings, perceptions, mental formations and consciousness—these factors are subject to cankers.

**Digest:**

Which factors are subject to (the influence of) cankers?

The wholesome states pertaining to the three (mundane) spheres, the unwholesome states, the resultant states pertaining to the three (mundane) spheres, the functional indeterminate states pertaining to the three spheres, and all corporeality, these factors are subject to cankers.

**Comment**

The word *sāsava* is exceedingly significant. As the object of the cankers, it falls within the domain or sway of the cankers. Therefore the range of the *āsava* is very wide indeed. The *anāsava* (canker-free) comprises the supramundane, while the *sāsava* (subject to cankers) includes the entire mundane realm. The supramundane canker-free-insight of the *Arahat* enables him to act as a catalyst. While he lives the life of an ordinary individual, his mind never comes within the range of the *āsavas*. On the other hand he greatly influences the lives of others and the world in a way to counter and destroy the *āsavas*.

Further, even a wholesome and inderminate phenomenon can be trapped within the snares of the *āsavas* by becoming their object. Thus the good too is a prey to the *āsavas*, since goodness by itself does not ensure the power of catalytic action. It is, of course, understandable that *akusalas* can always be feeders of further *akusalas*, and therefore be *āsavas*. But as to the sublime states, even supernormal attainments like absorptions and supernormal powers, short of the Supramundane, come within the influence of *āsavas*. That being the case, for spiritual seekers it should be a matter of concern and ought to create in them a sense of disenchantment and spiritual disgust with everything that is mundane.

Anything which acts as a condition, influences the mind and mundane phenomena, i.e. conditions the mind in a way to be within the realm of bondage, *saṃsāra*. For instance, a person performs a lot of charity, sincerely observes the moral precepts, meditates and cultivates the absorptions, and therewith acquires supernormal powers; he or she certainly has acquired excellence and is worthy of respect and acclamation. However, when this person exults in his or her virtue and is not only aware of the acquisitions but advertises them (as many miracle-men do), then these very sublime attainments defile the mind and lead to his or her downfall. This is how even the supernormal achievements, so long as one has not reached the supramundane, can always subject one to the machinations of the *āsavas*.

Just as Nibbāna is the object of all Supramundane Insights, mundane objects constitute the objects of all mundane states of consciousness. Everything in the mundane realm-*citta*, *cetasika*, *rūpa*, the five aggregates, *pañca-khandha*, whether of the past, of the present or of the future, can become objects of consciousness, particularly of the *akusala* states. That is why all mundane phenomena are *sāsava*, also called *papañca*, which means that which proliferates, becomes scattered, multiplies or ramifies, thus self-perpetuates and becomes differentiated in the process. In fact, it is because of this manifoldness and diffuseness of all mundane objects that they lead to discursiveness, dispersal of mental energy and distraction.

Nibbāna, in contradistinction is called *nippapañca*, the dimension of the undifferentiated, the cessation of diffusiveness. The relation between *sāsava* and *papañca* is a psychological actuality. As soon as one is placed in the world of manifoldness, one tends to be distracted by the sheer differentiation and diffusiveness of objects around. This leads automatically to a proliferation of concepts and ideas. The proliferation of concepts leads to the profuseness of conceptualizations and thereby to an overabundance of contentions.

Contentions lead to ethical problems, whether these are based on religious or secular matters. That is why the word *papañca* also means worldliness. A person who is too involved in acquisitiveness must struggle to defend what he acquires, and so, swinging between offence and defence, he has to tarry in the world, thus delaying the possibility of liberation. *Papañca,* therefore, also means delay, appropriately. From this threefold meaning of *papañca*, the implications of *sāsava* should be understood.

**Exposition**

Which factors are not subject to (i.e. are beyond the range of) cankers?

The supramundane path insights and fruition-insights, as well as the Unconditioned Element (Nibbāna dhātu)—these factors are not subject to cankers.

**Digest**

Which factors are not subject to (are beyond the range of) cankers?

The four supramundane path-insights, the four supramundane fruition insights, and Nibbāna—these factors are not subject to cankers.

**Comment**

*Apariyāpanna*, lit. *unincluded*, means that which is exempt from the mundane spheres and thereby from the cycles of birth, death and rebirth. When Nibbāna comes within the focus of consciousness, the mind gets automatically rid of the *āsāvas*. It is like darkness getting dispelled forthwith by the inflow of light, or malodour getting dispersed by fragrance, or waste material being consumed by fire. That is why Nibbāna is called *anāsava*, canker-freed, something which is itself void of cankers and which brings about the destruction of cankers.

The path and fruition-insigts are *anāsava* because they have been transformed into the Nibbānic element, by coming in contact with Nibbāna. The fruition-insight is significantly called the fruit of holiness (*sāmañña-phala*), because it is through this state that one plunges into the Unconditioned Element and remains there in the enjoyment of the bliss of emancipation arising therefrom.

**Exposition**

Which factors are associated with cankers?

Those factors which are associated with cankers are the aggregates of feelings, perceptions, mental formations and consciousness—these factors are associated with cankers.

**Digest**

Which factors are associated with cankers?

Except delusion, which arises concomitantly with the two states of consciousness rooted in hatred; except delusion, which arises together with the state of consciousness rooted in (lit. accompanied by) sceptical doubt, and the state of consciousness rooted in restlessness; the remaining unwholesome states (consciousness and their concomitants)—these are the factors that are associated with cankers.

**Comment**

Associated with cankers (*āsava-sampayutta*) means factors which go together and are conjoined with the cankers. These are the twelve *akusala cittas* and the ten *cetasikas*. There are fourteen *akusala cetasikas*, four of *which—moha*, *lobha* (= *kāma*), *māna* (= *bhava*) and *diṭṭhi*—are cankers, the remaining being the associates of the cankers. The cankers extant in the eight *lobha-mūlika cittas* are mutually dependent. In the four *dosa* and *moha-mūlika cittas* there is only one canker, namely, *moha*. *Moha* therefore is not a canker-associate, being itself a canker. In fact, it is called dissociated from cankers, i.e., disjoined from other cankers which do not occur in these four states of consciousness.

The psychological implications of *moha*, particularly with reference to anger, anxiety, restlessness, guilt, doubt, cynicism, etc., are indeed thought-provoking and revealing. *Moha* basically signifies mental blindness, and there are degrees of this blindness as in optical blindness. The colour-blind man is very different from the night-blind or the short-sighted. The handicaps connected with each of these types of blindness vary greatly. The mental blindness of an angry man is very different from that of a lustful or a cynical or distracted man. The specifics of this condition have been indicated specially by mentioning *moha* in these texts. A detailed study of this phenomenon could be most rewarding. After all, it is delusion (mental blindness) that is at the root of all troubles in the world. And an understanding of this alone can produce the solutions.

**Exposition**

Which factors are dissociated from cankers?

Those factors which are dissociated from the cankers are the aggregates of feelings, perceptions, mental formations and consciousness; all forms of corporeality, and the unconditioned element—these factors are dissociated from cankers.

**Digest**

Which factors are dissociated from cankers?

Delusion which arises together with the two states of consciousness rooted in hatred; delusion which arises together with (the state of consciousness rooted in) sceptical-doubt; delusion which arises together with (the state of consciousness rooted in) restlessness; the wholesome states pertaining to the four spheres; the resultant states pertaining to the four spheres; the functional-indeterminate states pertaining to the three spheres; corporeality and Nibbāna these are the factors that are dissociated from cankers.

**Comment**

Factors dissociated from cankers are the *kusalas*, *vipākas*, *kiriyās*, corporeality, Nibbāna, and as mentioned already, *moha* pertaining to *dosa* and *moha-mūlika cittas*. Except the supramundane, these phenomena, though dissociated from *āsavas*, yet being *sāsavas*, can always be affected by *āsavas*. The underlying idea is that one should never take things for granted. So long as one is within the domain of the mundane, one is always within the dominion of the *āsavas*, and one can always be dominated by *āsavas*.

**Exposition**

Which factors are both cankers, as well as subject to cankers?

These very cankers are (both) cankers, as well as subject to cankers.

**Digest**

Which factors are both cankers, as well as subject to cankers?

These very cankers are (both) cankers, as well as subject to cankers.

Comment

It is an interesting fact that the *āsavas* are also *sāsavas*. The truth of this relationship is that it effectively and efficiently maintains the feedback system. Bondage, after all, is created by the *āsava-sāsava* nexus.

**Exposition**

Which factors are subject to cankers, but are not (themselves) cankers?

Excluding the cankers from those factors which are subject to cankers, the remaining wholesome, unwholesome and indeterminate states that are subject to cankers, pertaining to the sphere of the sense-desire, the sphere of subtle form, and the immaterial sphere, namely, the aggregates of corporeality, feelings, perceptions, mental formations and consciousness —these factors are subject to cankers, but are not (themselves) cankers.

**Digest**

Which factors are subject to cankers, but are not (themselves) cankers?

Except the cankers, the remaining unwholesome states; the wholesome states pertaining to the three spheres; the resultant states pertaining to the three spheres; the functional-indeterminate states pertaining to the three spheres; all corporeality—these are the factors that are subject to cankers, but are not themselves cankers.

Factors that are not subject to cankers should not be construed as 'cankers as well as subject to cankers', or 'subject to cankers though not cankers (themselves).'

**Comment**

As already mentioned, *sāsavas* embrace the entire gamut of the 161 mundane phenomena (81 *cittas*. 52 *cetatikas*, 28 *rūpas*). Leaving the four *āsavas* out of these 161, the remaining 157 factors come within this enquiry of the truth. It is interesting to note that the text specifically mentions *anāsava* to be precluded from both the seventh and eighth enquiries. This is because the *anāsava*, being wholly transcendent, cannot be and should not be connected with the *sāsava*, which can be either canker or non-canker.

**Exposition**

Which factors are (both) cankers, as well as associated with cankers ?

The canker of desire for sense-pleasure in relation to the canker of ignorance, is a canker, as well as that which is associated with a canker; the canker of ignorance, in relation to the canker of desire for sense-pleasure, is a canker, as well as that which is associated with a canker; the canker of desire for the continuation of existence, with reference to the canker of ignorance is a canker, as well as that which is associated with a canker; the canker of ignorance, in relation to the canker of desire for the continuation of existence, is a canker, as well as that which is associated with a canker; the canker of wrong views, in relation to the canker of ignorance, is a canker, as well as that which is associated with a canker; the canker of ignorance, in relation to the canker of wrong views, is a canker, as well as that which is associated with a canker.

**Digest**

Which factors are (both) cankers, as well as associated with cankers?

When (in a state of consciousness) two or three cankers arise together, (then) these factors are both cankers, as well as associated with cankers.

**Comment**

In the *lobha-mūlika cittas* all the four *āsavas* occur in different combinations. In such situation they are both *āsavas* and *āsava-sampayuttas*.

**Exposition**

Which factors are associated with cankers, but are not (themselves) cankers?

Excluding cankers from those factors which are associated with cankers, namely, the aggregates of feelings, perceptions, mental formations and consciousness—these factors are associated with cankers, but are not (themselves) cankers.

**Digest**

Which factors are associated with cankers, but are not (themselves) cankers?

Except the cankers, (all) the remaining unwholesome states—these factors are associated with cankers, though not cankers (themselves).

**Comment**

This refers to the twelve *akusala cittas* and the twenty three *cetasikas* – which accompany the *āsavas*.

The four *āsavas* are present only in the twelve unwholesome states of consciousness and the twenty-seven mental factors (13 common type and 14 unwholesome type) This means that factors which are not *āsavas*, but which are associated with them, are the twelve *akusala cittas*, unwholesome states of consciousness, and the twenty-three *cetasikas,* mental factors (27- 4=23).

A state of consciousness is unwholesome or wholesome because of its concomitant mental factors. *Āsavas,* as mental factors, are also roots (*hetus*) that determine the unwholesome nature of the consciousness. The twelve *akusala cittas* belong to the aggregate of consciousness, *vinñāṇa-khandha*, while the 27 *cetasikas* constitute the aggregates of feelings (*vedanā*), perceptions (*saññā*), and mental formations (*saṇkhāra*). *Vedanā* and *saññā* cetasikas belong to the 13 common type while the rest 25 of the 27 mental factors belong to the *saṇkhāra khandha*. That they are both *cetasikas* and *khandhas* only underline their predominant role. In the Exposition section, the answer is given in terms of the *khandhas*, while the Digest section makes a general summarization.

**Exposition**

Which factors are dissociated from cankers, but are subject to cankers?

Those factors that are dissociated from the cankers are the wholesome, the unwholesome and the indeterminate states, which are subject to cankers and which belong to the sphere of the sense-desire, the sphere of subtle form, and the formless sphere, and the aggregates of corporeality, feelings, perceptions, mental formations and consciousness; these factors are dissociated from cankers, but are subject to cankers.

**Digest**

Which factors are dissociated from cankers, but are subject to cankers?

Delusion which arises together with the two states of consciousness rooted in hatred; delusion which arises together with (the state of consciousness accompanied by) sceptical doubt; delusion which arises together with (the state of consciousness accompanied by) restlessness; the wholesome states pertaining to the three spheres; the resultant states pertaining to the three spheres; the functional-indeterminate states pertaining to the three spheres ; and all corporeality—these are the factors that are dissociated from cankers, but are subject to cankers.

**Comment**

Delusion (*moha)* as the root of 4 akusala cittas, (2 *dosa* rooted and 2 *moha* rooted), 17 *kusala* cittas of the 3 spheres, 32 *vipāka* cittas of 3 spheres, 20 *kriya* cittas of 3 spheres, ( 1+17+32+20+28=98) these 98 mundane phenomena are the factors which although are dissociated, yet are subject to cankers.

**Exposition**

Which are the factors that are dissociated from cankers, and also not subject to cankers?

The supramundane path-insights and the fruition-insights, as well as the Unconditioned Element—these 9 factors are dissociated from cankers, and also not subject to cankers.

**Digest**

Which factors are dissociated from cankers, and also not subject to cankers?

The four supramundane path-insights, the four supramundane fruition-insights of the holy life *(Sāmañña phala)*, and Nibbāna—these 9 factors are dissociated from cankers and also not subject to cankers.

Factors associated with cankers should not be construed as 'dissociated from and subject to cankers,' or 'dissociated from, and not subject to cankers.'

**Comment**

The supramundane insights and Nibbāna, these nine *dhammas* being dissociated from cankers, and being canker-free, constitute the only dimension of security and peace. Mere dissociation does not ensure emancipation from cankers; only when the dissociation is combined with transformation resulting from destruction of cankers, that the canker-free state of the Arahat is achieved. The twelve *akusala-cittas* and the thirteen *cetasikas* associated with the cankers have been definitely excluded from these two categories of enquiry (11 and 12). Hence the phrase, 'should not be construed as dissociated from, etc.'

# Chapter 24

## THE WORTHY ONE

*The Qualities of the Canker-free*

Herewith are presented the qualities, of the canker-free enlightened being, the Arahat, who is the Perfect One, therefore the Worthy One.

It is a most edifying experience for a seeker of truth to know how the Canker-free Ones behave, in their day-to-day lives so that the seeker may some day become one of them, by emulating their conduct. A journey of a million miles starts with the first step and however exalted this exalted state of spirituality is, by aiming at it, one day the journey will surely be completed. However imperfect one's conduct be at the beginning, by following in the footsteps of these great ones, one is ensured of this final triumph.

The chapter on the Worthy One, *Arahantavagga,* in the *Dhammapada*, is an inspiring one. It reveals in clear terms the qualities of the Arahat, the Canker-free one. The Arahat has no equal in the world, because he has transcended the world, he is no longer subject to *kamma* and rebirth. Therefore, he alone is the ideal individual, exemplifying the highest goal, and his attainments, as the true model, are worthy of emulation.

## THE WORTHY

*The fever of passion exists not*
*For him who has completed the journey,*
*Who is sorrowless and wholly set free,*
*And who has broken all ties.* Dhp 90

*Always mindful, they are ever active;*
*They are not attached to any abode.*
*Like swans that abandon the lake,*
*They leave abode after abode behind.* Dhp 91

*Those who accumulate not*
*And are wise regarding food.*
*Whose object is the The Void,*
*The Unconditioned Freedom*
*Their track cannot be traced*
*Like that of birds in the air* Dhp 92

*He whose cankers are destroyed,*
*Who is not attached to food,*
*Whose object is the The Void,*
*The Unconditioned Freedom—*
*His path cannot be traced,*
*Like that of birds in the air.* Dhp 93

*Even the gods hold dear the wise ones,*
*Whose senses are subdued,*
*Like horses well-trained by a charioteer;*
*Whose pride is destroyed,*
*And is free from cankers.* Dhp 94

*There is no more worldly existence for the wise one,*
*Who, like the earth, resents nothing;*
*Who is as firm as a high pillar*
*And as pure as a deep pool free from mud.* Dhp 95

*Calm is his thought,*
*Calm his word*
*And calm his deed–*
*Who truly knowing is wholly freed,*
*And perfectly tranquil and wise.* Dhp 96

*The man who is without blind faith,*
*Who knows the Uncreated,*
*Who has severed all links,*
*Who has destroyed all causes (for kamma)*
*And who has thrown out all desires*
*He truly is the most excellent of men.* Dhp 97

*Inspiring, indeed, is that place*
*Where the Arahats dwell,*
*Be it a village or a forest,*
*A vale or a hill.* Dhp 98

*Inspiring are the forests*
*in which worldlings find no pleasure.*
*There the passionless will rejoice,*
*For, they seek no sensual pleasures.* Dhp 99

Thirty-seven specific qualities of a *khināsava* have been enumerated in the afore-mentioned ten verses, *gatiddhino* being the first attribute.

Life according to Buddhism is a journey, *addhaṃ.* Now a journey can be an aimless wandering or a very elevating pilgrimage. In a dichotomous world everything is characterised by this innate duality. Wisdom lies in opting for the positive, edifying and onward-leading, despite all the hardships that may have to be undergone.

After all. whatever is hard to achieve is worth achieving and to be the Worthy of Worthies, one must choose only the difficult and therefore the worthy path. To give in to the way of the world is easy, being cheap and unworthy. The Arahats do not choose the cheap way, but pay the highest price to complete the journey *(gatiddhino),* of transcending *saṃsāra.*

The Arahat is also called 'sorrowless.' Being the very embodiment of equanimity, he has outgrown the dualities that grief, sorrow, despair, dejection, sadness and such states of distress and anguish occasion. Sorrow is the profile, in sharp outline, of a scorched mental condition, born of loss or frustration. It is derived from the root *suc,* which means to burn or scorch.

When somebody loses a dear one or a precious thing, or contrarily, when one fails to achieve one's desires, the mind is heated up, so to say, and is burnt, the pain whereof is expressed as grief, sorrow etc. Since the Arahat seeks nothing, he also loses nothing. Therefore, he is the Sorrowless, the Happy One.

The Arahat is called *vippamutta,* wholly set free, because he is liberated not only from human limitations but also from divine ones, and this is highlighted by the attribute *sabbagantha-ppahīno,* 'who has broken all ties.'

*Saṃsāra* is characterized by the fever of passion. The fever is a telling analogy indeed and the Arahat who has succeeded in turning the destructive heat of fever into a burning zeal of supramundane accomplishment has therefore performed the most marvellous feat.

It is sometimes asked, when an Arahat has achieved the highest, where is the need for him to exert further? The Arahat's efforts are symptomatic of the zeal he so abundantly has, and which he employs to exemplify the Dhamma. The Arahat is ever active, *uyyuñjati,* 'for the happiness of the many, for the welfare of the many.' His effort thus is concomitant with his compassion and altruism, and since he embodies the Dhamma and exemplifies it, and is also actively engaged in promoting it, he is ever-mindful.

If mundane existence is marked by the craving to enjoy, the supramundane attainments are distinguished by savouring of the freedom and bliss. However, the craze for pleasures and possessions inevitably brings turmoil, while the supramundane is characterized by its inherent peace and tranquillity. While the worldling, fettered to his world, delights in and is attached to his home etc., the Arahat, with his total detachment and dispassion, rejoices in the freedom of homelessness and emancipation from the sense of belonging. Hence the analogy, 'like swans that abandon the lakes, they leave abode after abode behind.'

It is obvious therefore that the source of true happiness lies not in accumulation, nor in enjoyment of food, pleasure, or any worldly thing, but in detachment. Therefore the Buddha has said that even a place, be it a village or a forest, a valley or a hill, where the Arahats dwell is delightful because there the worldlings do not find anything to take pleasure in. The passionless rejoice in their abode because they seek no sensual pleasure.

The Arahats also make use of all the requisites necessary for living, like food, or a place to stay ; but then, they do it with wisdom, and therefore are emancipated from them, unlike the worldling. Since they are not attached to anything, they don't acquire any *kamma* wherewith to lay the track of future becoming. They are like birds in the air, leaving no trail.

The trail or track analogy also stands for a given plane of existence. After the Arahat passes into final deliverance *(parinibbāna),* it is impossible to track the trackless path of the Arahat, as with the birds in the air. Hence, the attribute, *durannayaṃ*. His destiny (*gati)* is beyond knowledge refers to the supramundane dimension of liberation, which is wholly unlike that of the mundane. In the track-ridden sphere of the mundane there is nothing by which the supramundane can be compared or described.

The Arahat only resorts to the *vimokkhas* or deliverances. This subject has been already treated (see Canker and Deliverance page . . .) It is the resort to deliverance that turns the consciousness of the Arahat into what is called *tādī*, dwelling in 'suchness', that is, the truth leading to the canker-free *anāsava* state.

Since the 'Suchness' (*tādī*) is totally settled and equipoised, he is like the earth, which neither resents nor rejoices. He is 'as firm as a high pillar' *(indakhīla),* and 'as pure as the deep pool free from mud'. These similes are exceedingly apt for whom there is no more *saṃsāra.*

The qualities of equipoise and tranquillity make the Arahat dear even to the gods. He is the perfect example of self-restraint. Calm in his thought, word and deed, and with senses well subdued, he is compared to a noble horse that has been perfectly tamed and trained by a great charioteer. The Arahat's self-mastery is a reflection of his freedom from the cankers, pride, etc. He is called, therefore, one who, truly knowing, is wholly freed–*sammadañña vimutto.*

The Arahat can never be compared to anybody or anything of the world, however sublime. Gods of the various divine planes are undoubtedly exalted, in that they enjoy immense power and bliss. Many human beings even regard them to be almighty. And compared with the life span of human beings, the immensely long life of hundreds and thousands of aeons, not years, would certainly appear to be eternal. But the gods, whether written in capital or small letters, also belong to the mundane sphere and are subject to the law of moral causation, *kamma*, and therefore undergo rebirth. Since the Arahat has transcended everything mundane, has broken the vicious circle of *kamma* and rebirth, and has found access unto the transmundane, he is superior to all gods. An Arahat can be either a human or a divine being. In fact, there are innumerable gods who have attained to this exalted state of perfection, and therefore whose protection is ever available to all the votaries of the holy Triple Gem—the Buddha, the Dhamma and the Sangha.

In this chapter, verse 97, is intriguing because of a deliberate use of terms having double-meaning, one rather scandalous, and the other sublime. These conundrums are *asaddho*, literally, faithless. But in the case of the Arahat it means without blind faith, because the Arahat has an unshakeable faith in what he directly experiences, namely, the supramundane insights and Nibbāna. Since the Arahat truly knows, he is naturally freed from blind faith.

*Akataññu* literally means one who does not know or acknowledge the good done; that is, an ungrateful or thankless man. In this context, it means the one who knows the Uncreated (*akataññu*= un (*a*-) + made or created (*kata*) + knower (*-ññu*). The idea is that the Arahat, having reached the highest state of spirituality, has realized Nibbāna, the uncreated (*akata*). Nibbāna is called uncreated because it is beyond the vicious circle of *kamma* and rebirth. *Saṃsāra*, a synonym of this circle, signifies a continuous creation which is endless and meaningless. Uncreated means something existing but not created. So Nibbāna exists without being created by anyone or anything.

This mundane sphere is characterised by an endless creativity based upon various mundane laws, physical, biological, moral and mental. In contradistinction, the supramundane is the opposite of the involvement and turmoil innate in creativity. The quintessential character of the transmundane is peace and tranquillity. If life and the world are created by volition, Nibbāna transcends all volitional activity and creativity. Therefore, unlike *saṃsāra*, it has no beginning and no end. It has not been created by any force or agency, and has no underlying support like a godhead etc. and it is wholly unconditioned.

In the celebrated passage found in the *Udāna* (8.3), the

Buddha clearly enunciated that if such an unconditioned and uncreated dimension of freedom were not there, liberation from the mundane would not be possible. Since there is the uncreated, and there are the knowers of the uncreated, deliverance from the bondage of the mundane becomes a reality.

*Sandhicchedo*, literally, a housebreaker. In this context it means one who has severed all links, that is, who has broken open the house designed by craving and built by *kamma*. This riddlesome expression highlights those factors by which the wheel of becoming is continuously kept moving, as enunciated by the Buddha in his teaching of the *paṭicca-samuppāda*, Dependent Origination of all existence.

The term *hatāvakāso*, literally means: one who spoils opportunities or the occasions to gain etc. In this context it means one who has destroyed all occasions for good and evil, and therewith the vicious circle of *kamma* and rebirth. Since the Arahat gives no room for the perpetuation of bondage, he is a killer *(hata)* of occasions (*avakāso)*. Having thrown out all desires by means of the highest supramundane path-insight, and therewith having become one without blind faith, as the knower of the uncreated, the breaker of the house called *saṃsāra* and the occasion-killer, he alone is the most exalted of men, *uttama puriso;* the passionless, *vītarāga*, who never seeks anything to please the senses.

This riddle-ridden verse was pronounced by the Buddha on a very controversial issue, in which his own chief disciple, the Venerable Sāriputta was involved. When the Buddha was staying at the Jetavana monastery, thirty monks who were forest-dwellers engaged in intense spiritual practice visited the Master to pay their reverence. Focusing his attention, the Lord discerned their potential for becoming Arahats and acquiring all the supernatural powers.

He wanted to emphasize the need for bringing to maturity the five spiritual faculties of Faith (*saddhā*), Effort (*viriya*), Mindfulness (*sati*) Meditative Concentration (*samādhi*) and

Wisdom (*paññā*), leading to the destruction of the cankers, and therewith the attainment of the deathless state of Nibbāna. These thirty hermit monks were already ripe. They had cultivated their faculties fully, and all they needed was a spiritual boost in the form of a discourse from the sacred lips of the Blessed One.

The Buddha, with a measure of deliberateness, put a question to Venerable Sāriputta, who was also seated in the congregation. Said the Buddha: ''Sāriputta, do you believe that, when fully developed and repleatedly practised, the spiritual faculty of faith leads to the Deathless, converges on the Deathless?'' He also repeated the same question with reference to the remaining four spiritual faculties.

Answered Venerable Sāriputta: ''Most Venerable Sir, I do not go into this matter by faith in the Blessed One's enunciation, namely, 'When fully developed and repeatedly practised, the spiritual faculty of faith leads to the Deathless, converges on the Deathless.' Most Venerable Sir, those by whom the Deathless is not known, not seen, not understood, not realized and not experienced through intuitive insight, it would be all right for them to go by faith in others that 'When fully developed and repleatedly practised, the spiritual faculty of faith leads to the Deathless, converges on the Deathless.'

Now, some monks, who could not understand the implication of this dialogue turned this into a controversial issue. Some of them, who were envious of the great saint Sāriputta, being given such a pre-eminent place in the Dispensation by the Master and being highly respected by the large circle of disciples, both monastic and lay. They went about spreading this canard;'' Well, the Elder Sāriputta has not yet given up his old wrong views. He does not have faith even today in the supremely Enlightened One.''

When the Master came to know of this slanderous accusation, He asked them, ''Monks, why do you go about saying this? After all, what I implied when I asked him was this: 'Well Sāriputta, do you believe that without developing these five spiritual faculties, without cultivating the two systems of meditation, namely, tranquillity *(samatha)* and insight *(vipassanā)*, is it ever possible for anyone to realize the supramundane path and fruition-insights'? What he answered was, 'Most Venerable Sir, I don't believe that there is ever the possibility for anyone to so realize.' By this it is clear that he does not believe in such a ripening and fruition when the person has not fulfilled the prerequisites by way of practising alms-offering and fulfilling various deeds of merit. Not that he does not believe in the qualities of virtues of the Enlightened One and of his holy disciples. All that he meant was that he does not merely, out of credulity, go by others' words. But what has been enunciated by the Buddha is a sacrosanct truth to him, by virtue of the fact that he himself has, by his own intuitive wisdom, penetrated to it, having himself attained to the various spiritual and supernatural attainments, such as the meditative absorptions, all the stages of insight-meditation, and the supramundane path and fruition insights leading to Nibbāna. Therefore, he is not open 'to any censor.'

Then the Exalted One analysed and pieced together the various aspects. Thereafter he gave a discourse, and pronounced this verse in conclusion:

The man who is without blind faith,
Who knows the uncreated,
Who has severed all links,
Who has destroyed all occasions,
And who has thrown out all desires-
He, truly, is the most excellent of men. Dhp. 97

End